THE HEROINE'S JOURNEY

THE HEROINE'S JOURNEY

For Writers, Readers, and Fans of Pop Culture

GAIL CARRIGER

G A I L C A R R I G E R, L L C

Copyright © 2020 by GAIL CARRIGER LLC
Cover © 2020 by GAIL CARRIGER LLC, assembled by Starla Huchton,
designedbystarla.com

Version 1.0
eBook ISBN 978-1-944751-50-0
Print ISBN 978-1-944751-34-0

I have been truly blessed over my lifetime with some wonderful teachers, but Thomas Van Nortwick of the Oberlin Classics Department was one of the very best. So this book is dedicated to the man who got me started on my journey.

Thank you for showing me how to rip off my crown and descend from Mount Olympus… okay, that didn't come out quite right.

How about this?

In a typical withdrawal and return pattern, I have come back around to your teaching, twenty-odd years later, never realizing that I was making use of it all along.

Mr V – I did not turn out to be the classical archaeologist professor that perhaps we all expected. To be fair, I was never going to pass Latin with flying colors. Nevertheless, words cannot express my profound gratitude for the four years of education you gave me.

Do teachers know they change people's lives and start them on new adventures? I hope so.

Thank you for being the mentor-who-is-friend on my Heroine's Journey.

CONTENTS

CHAPTER 5: HEROINE'S JOURNEY BEATS, THEMES & MESSAGES

CHAPTER 6: HEROINE'S JOURNEY GETS DEVALUED

CHAPTER 7: GENRE COMPLICATIONS

CHAPTER 8: NARRATIVE VARIATIONS

CHAPTER 9: READER EXPERIENCE

CHAPTER 10: HOW TO WRITE LIKE A HEROINE

INTRODUCTION

The Heroine's Journey

The Heroine's Journey is a separate narrative structure from the Hero's Journey. It exists. It has always existed. It is not derivative of, nor sourced in, the Hero's Journey. I thought, for a really long time, that everyone knew this.

I was wrong.

Which is how I (a fiction writer) have ended up writing this nonfiction book.

They say that the oldest trick for nonfiction is threefold:

1. Tell them what you're doing.
2. Do it.
3. Tell them what you did.

Truth? Exactly the same thing works for dirty talk, if you're writing a sex scene... or just in life. (See what I did there? Now you know what kind of book this is.)

So I shall tell you, right up front, the basics of the Heroine's Journey and how it compares to the Hero's Journey.

Then I'll provide evidence for those basics using ancient myth and modern pop culture. Then I'll break them all down so you can use them yourself. Finally, I'll remind you of what I told you from the get-go. Knowledge: the best kind of dirty talk.

To get us started on the right path, so to speak:

HERE IS THE HERO'S JOURNEY IN ONE PITHY SENTENCE:

Increasingly isolated protagonist stomps around prodding evil with pointy bits, eventually fatally prods baddie, gains glory and honor.

HERE IS THE HEROINE'S JOURNEY IN ONE PITHY SENTENCE:

Increasingly networked protagonist strides around with good friends, prodding them and others on to victory, together.

Don't worry, more (considerably less flippant) definitions of both of these are yet to come.

However, I have been told not to be coy and to just lay it out there for you from the beginning.

Consider it laid.

Essentially the Heroine's Journey is different from the Hero's Journey in five significant storytelling ways (also known as the Five Key Ingredients):

1. PURPOSE

The goal or focus of the journey is different. A hero is usually concerned with defeating an enemy or retrieving a boon of great import – think classic video game quests.

A heroine is looking for reunification with someone who was taken from her. She is concerned with networking, connecting with others, and finding family.

2. APPROACH

A hero acts on the offensive most of the time. He is active in his pursuit of his goal and will kill or (in the case of Odysseus) trick his way to victory. His enemy is stasis.

A heroine goes about achieving her goals through communication and information gathering. She is not a conqueror. She is a builder and a general – she sees the skills and strengths in others and knows how best to apply them. She is a delegator, which is great for storytellers because it's easy to build vibrant, supportive, extremely appealing side characters. Also, this humanizes the protagonist, who is self-aware enough to know what she is good at and when someone else can do it better.

Her enemy is loneliness or isolation.

3. STRENGTH

A heroine's definition of strength is materially different from that of the hero. A hero must eventually go it alone; the journey usually climaxes with a one-on-one defeat of his enemy. For him, asking for help is a sign of weakness.

He must shed the restrictions of civilization and family in order to succeed on his own.

A heroine is the opposite. Requesting aid is a sign of strength. It does not diminish a heroine to seek and receive assistance on her journey. In fact, the more companions she has, the stronger she is.

(And if that concept makes you wince, perhaps you might consider your own personal definition of what *strength* means and how the narratives around you have influenced that.)

4. POWER

As a result of all the above, when a heroine has her most powerful narrative and iconic moments, these will occur *with others*. They are usually characterized by intense communication and unity in the context of sex, romance, friendship, or familial relationships.

When the hero is at his most powerful, he is alone, because his quest is one of self-reliance and solitary achievement against overwhelming odds. His iconic moments will be ones of intellectual or physical superiority over someone else.

5. ENDING

A hero, because of his need to self-isolate, has sacrificed too much for his goal, so the end of his journey is bitter-sweet. Iconography often depicts him alone, with the slow pan-out sequence and a sense of profound pathos. He has either grown too powerful to fit back into the world he has saved, or he has changed too much into a solo version of himself and can no longer exist in a group.

Poignancy typifies the end of a heroic narrative – lonely death, hard drinking, a hermit's existence.

The heroine is more likely to get a happy ending, surrounded by friends and family, with an implication of continued safety.

FOLLOW-UPS TO THE FIVE KEY INGREDIENTS

The above are some broad brush strokes, but I'm giving you the essentials before we tunnel into specifics. In other words, these are the five explanations I trot out at cocktail parties. (Yes, I go to the type of gatherings where we chat about the Heroine's Journey.)

One important note:

Biological sex characteristics are irrelevant to whether a main character is a hero or a heroine.

In other words, women, female-identified, and nonbinary characters can be heroes. Men, male-identified, and nonbinary characters can be heroines.

And one note of caution:

We humans have a tendency (once we know the two different journeys) to want to pigeonhole and fit every story we encounter into one model or the other. We like the binary; it's simple and fun. Things are rarely that black and white – for readers or creators.

My idea is to teach storytellers a basic understanding of the two models, so you learn when to obey the narrative beats and when to break them, in order to better manage reader expectations.

Similarly, I hope to educate the consumers of such stories, so they can better understand their own desires.

Please, try not to use these two journeys to pigeonhole every piece of pop culture you encounter. Therein lies madness.

Yes, many stories do fit into one journey or the other, but not all of them (I'm looking at you, *Black Panther*, 2018). I'll be talking about the havoc that swapped point of view narratives, buddy dramas, and ensemble casts can play with fitting comfortably into one or the other journey later on in this book.

To be clear, you've read the Heroine's Journey in its many forms before. You've watched it. You just might not have realized that. More fascinating, perhaps? There's a good chance that you love it, even yearn for more.

I intend to show you how to activate your own version of this narrative, whether as a writer of fiction, scripts, and games; as a parent thoughtfully choosing books for a child; or as a reader trying to better understand your own tastes and preferences.

This book will leave you with a solid working knowledge of how to read, identify, and understand what makes a Heroine's Journey, and from there, how to write a good one.

CHAPTER 1: APPROACH

Why the table of contents looks the way it does

I've given you lots of chapter headings and pithy subtitles, because even in my nonfiction I love this kind of thing, but also so you can skip around and read what interests you.

I'm going to start by providing a foundation of shared terms and vocabulary. This is so that when I use a word like *theme* you know what *theme* means to me. I tend to find that semantics are the source of most major misunderstandings in life (well, that and instruction manuals for DIY furniture).

After a foundation of terminology, I'll provide an overview of the Hero's Journey. Since most writers already have a basic understanding of the Hero's Journey, I'd like to show you my view of it, and how my writer's perspective might be different (and different from the mainstay of Jungian and mythological analysis).

Then I will retell three core goddess-based ancient myths as a foundation for understanding the Heroine's Journey narrative beats and themes. These are:

1. Demeter (Ancient Greek)
2. Isis (Ancient Egyptian)
3. Inanna (Sumerian) or Ishtar (Akkadian and Assyrian)

With these first parts as a framework, I will then dive deep into the beats, themes, tropes, archetypes, function, and messaging of the Heroine's Journey. This will provide the tools you need to identify gendered themes and messages in your own work, the work of others, and the world around you.

We'll then explore the critical, social, and academic disenfranchisement of the Heroine's Journey and contrast that to its commercial success. The vilification of the romance genre is a prime example of wide-scale abuse of the Heroine's Journey. As is the disregard of comedy as frivolous or the trivialization of happy endings as pat, weak, unrealistic, or cheap.

We'll finish with a step-by-step actionable breakdown of what aspects of the Heroine's Journey make for a compelling narrative and how they might be applied, with examples and concrete tips. In other words, how the Heroine's Journey can be used to manipulate reader expectations and rule the entertainment world!

WHY DID I BOTHER?

In which I make some startling confessions

So how did a fiction writer end up taking on the grave risk of writing nonfiction?

Well, as stories are my wheelhouse, I'm going to start with a bit of one. However, I promise that *this* story is true.

> *Picture in your head a lady with a keen interest in classical mythology and philosophy, a passion for archaeology, and a side habit as a chronic fantasy author. If you want a visual, there is long brown hair in a scraggly ponytail, boot-cut jeans, and a propensity for green ribbed bodysuits – hey, it's the 90s.*

Sooo, in case you hadn't guessed, that's me. Long story short, I graduated with honors in archaeology and minors in theology, geology, anthropology, philosophy, and classics - and several unfinished fantasy novels. Yes, big ol' nerd. I really like learning, plus one tends to pick up lots of minors when one is an interdisciplinary major.

Still, I must confess that the last time I officially studied the Heroine's Journey was in school. But here's the thing: The moment I did study it, I noticed how much I was drawn to this narrative.

I found something profoundly comforting and reassuring in the connections a heroine makes, in her acts of solidarity, in the hope she renders, and in the gathering of information (or, occasionally, body parts – looking at you, Isis).

I'm not one of those people who thinks in terms of revenge. I don't want to go out by myself and chop off heads. This seems messy and lonely, and it never ends well, for either the chopper or the choppee. So clearly the Hero's Journey was not for me.

I wanted to read and write about family (found or otherwise) and go questing in the company of others. By all means, let's do the thing! But let's do that thing *together*. Learning to compromise might seem boring, but frankly, it also seems a darn sight more sensible and mature – and certainly more applicable to my own life.

So there I was, profoundly attracted to this particular narrative.

The Heroine's Journey was (and is) the kind of story that I enjoyed reading, watching, and writing, and yet when I left school and moved out into the world, *nobody seemed to know about it*. Not critics, not pop culture enthusiasts, not my fellow writers. Or if they did, they certainly didn't seem inclined to discuss the tropes, archetypes, and plots in the same way that everyone seems to with the Hero's Journey.

This felt odd to me. As if there were a conspiracy to hide away the good stuff, or to trivialize the Heroine's Journey to such an extent that I actually felt mildly embarrassed about my love for this particular narrative.

I'll say it now and I'll say it proud:

I like when things end happily, and most of the time that means, to me, *together*. I enjoy it when characters end up in solidarity, friends or family, lovers or platonic. That's what I hunt for... connection.

Because I love the Heroine's Journey, I started looking for it in the world around me. Not only in the books I read, but also in the movies and television I watched, the stories we tell each other, even the ways we build our own identities and priorities.

And here's the thing – the Heroine's Journey (as I lay it out in this book) is *endemic* to western culture.

This narrative, with its intentional themes and accidental messages, shows up all over. It bubbles up as stories of found families, and building loyalty, and co-adventure, and deep love. It surrounds us. It's in romance novels, buddy comedies, and cozy mysteries (cozies). It's the foundation for two of the bestselling series of all time (Harry Potter and *The Twilight Saga*).

I, for one, can't stop seeing this journey. I want to talk about it, I want to shout about it, but every time I start talking excitedly about the Heroine's Journey, someone says to me...

What?

What is this Heroine's Journey of which you speak?

What are you talking about?

Flash forward a couple of decades and, accidentally, I've stopped practicing archaeology and have become a best-selling author instead.

This is still the kind of story that I write, watch, and read. This journey is still necessary to me on a deep emotional and personal level, and still important to the world around me because of what it says about that world and its positive possibilities. It's vital to readers, watchers, and listeners of narrative.

And yet, when I say,

> "Oh, how lovely – that's a Heroine's Journey, that is! Hooray!"

People still reply with,

> "What's that? I mean, I know about the Hero's Journey, but what's the Heroine's? How is it different?"

Ten years as a Proper Author-Beast, and as I went on book tours, as I taught classes, as I sat on panels, as I discussed books with readers and librarians and booksellers, I started mentioning the Heroine's Journey.

And *every single time*, someone asked me to explain what that meant.

I believe that it's possible to learn to write the Heroine's Journey, to spot it, to understand it, and to send it back out into the world for fun and profit. The judicious use of some beats (if not all) allows storytellers to simultaneously satisfy their audience and keep them on their toes.

Studying the placement of this journey in history and modern culture allows us to understand both critical bias and audience cravings. Not to mention the fact that combining fiction skills with a conscious advocacy of the Heroine's Journey may, just possibly, alter modern perceptions of its worth and validity and our own need for sympathetic connection.

WHY SHOULD YOU BOTHER?

Storytellers need the Heroine's Journey

Ever come across that moment when your characters just won't act in the way you want them to? Your story is fighting you? Your plot feels stymied? The pacing seems off? It may be that you think you have scribbled your way along one journey, only you're actually writing the other.

As a reader, have you ever felt betrayed by a book, then jumped online to read reviews, only to discover that everyone else does too? Have you had the same thing occur with a TV show or a movie? It may be that everyone hates the ending of that one book because the author led readers to believe it was one journey and then swapped it at the last minute for another.

It's these kinds of pitfalls I'm hoping to guide you through.

This book should give creators the tools needed to spot the Heroine's Journey in modern pop culture wherever and whenever it appears, and analyze its success (or failure).

I intend to train your brain so you never look at pop culture the same way again.

What interests me is theming and messaging.

What can we writers learn from the Heroine's Journey about how to best tell a story? How can that knowledge allow us to better influence reader expectations and engender emotional responses in our audience?

What we have with both journeys is a narrative chassis. They have become models of how a story is *meant to be told*. Deviating from the model, or sticking closely to it, allows storytellers to tap into the unconscious yearning of an audience. We can understand a reader's resistance to one journey or another (or, indeed, our own). The sense of betrayal experienced by a viewer of, for example, the ending to *Battlestar Galactica* (2004 reboot) has to do not only with characters being untrue to their arcs, but also with the narrative being untrue to its initial journey.

Frankly, if we storytellers know both the Heroine's and the Hero's Journey, we are better able to control, manipulate, and capitalize on reader expectations. Simply put, we become *better* storytellers.

Why else do we write but to make people feel, and perhaps even think a little?

In more practical terms, understanding these journeys allows writers to:

- improve storytelling craft;
- tease out nuances of the writing process;

- manage (and manipulate) the audience experience; and
- use the power of narrative to bring about social change.

So, buckle up, muscle down, and let me entertain you with some truly fascinating nonfiction. Let's do this... together!

Like heroines.

POP CULTURE IS A WEAKNESS

Some things I hope you know before we start

During the course of this book, I'll be using pop culture as a quick shorthand reference for common shared modern narratives and experiences.

I will paraphrase and relay the core Heroine's Journeys that I used to form my breakdown (**Chapter 4**), but that's because I'm not sure how familiar you are with these myths.

I'm going to assume, however, that you have at least a passing familiarity with the following:

- Batman (the DC superhero character)
- *Battlestar Galactica* (reboot TV series from 2004)
- *Dangerous Liaisons* (1988 movie but other versions will do)
- *Dune* (books or movies)
- *A Song of Ice and Fire* (series of books) or *Game of Thrones* (TV series)
- Harry Potter (books or movies)
- *The Lord of the Rings* (books or movies)

- Sherlock Holmes (the fictional detective)
- Spider-Man (the Marvel superhero character)
- *Star Trek* (the 1966 original and 1987 next generation)
- *Star Wars* (original three movies)
- *The Twilight Saga* (books or movies)
- *Wonder Woman* (2017 movie)

This book should still make sense if you don't know something (or several somethings) on this list. But you will get more out if it, if you know a little about the above.

For your convenience (and entertainment), the back of this book includes not only my citations but additional information on most every representative of pop culture that I touch on in this text, as well as any snarky thoughts I have on the subject. This is meant to enlighten and amuse, but is mostly because I have never learned to hold my tongue and I'm a bad academic who does not believe in the sanctity of references.

CHAPTER 2: DEFINING TERMS

Getting academic

To start off, I'm getting all academic all over this stuff. Or something. Please bear with me. I know it's going to sound a bit dry, but it's important and interesting. You see, we really need to know the proper names for things; that way we can control them. There are fantasy magical systems that trade on that idea. It works for terms that illuminate story structure too.

My background is in social science and classical analysis, so I talk about mythology (as a writer) with a comparative (and to some extent, social) anthropological approach. In other words, I'm interested in the intersection between culture as a whole, and how we talk about and parlay myths as models of human behavior on a societal level. And from there, how use of the elements of myth manipulates story.

I am not interested in Jungian archetypal theory. In other words, I do not particularly care to examine myth as an example of internal personal journeys, nor to use it for psychological analysis. For one thing, these views tend to be based on early research that was pretty terrible about unconsciously associating biological sex and gender, and any anthropologist or classicist worth their salt will tell you these are *not the same thing*.

Speaking of which, gender needs to be addressed because it impacts the nature of perception around the conflict (amongst literary and pop-culture critics in particular) between the two journeys.

My aim is to address story themes and how they are perceived through the use of gendered tropes and archetypes, and how these are warped into culture-wide messages. Because we authors can control these messages, we need to understand the gendering that underpins and, occasionally, undermines them.

- So, what exactly do I mean by *gendered tropes and archetypes*?
- By *messages*?
- What is my definition of literary *themes*?

Terms, you see? It all comes down to terminology.

Thus I must define my terms for you, so that when I use a word, there's as much clarity as possible in understanding what I mean by that word in this book. A sort of nonfiction world building, if you will.

IT'S ALL ABOUT SEX & GENDER

Honestly, isn't everything?

So far as terms are concerned, I'd like to start with *sex* and *gender*. Because of course I do.

So... Gender and biological sex are *not the same thing*.

In this section, I'm going to discuss how we anthropologists go about defining the difference. The difference between these two terms is so incredibly important to our understanding of the Heroine's Journey (and how it is distinguished from the Hero's) that I've devoted a whole section to it and honestly, if you read nothing else in this book, please read this bit.

First, I must say that even as I apply this analysis technique, I'm aware there are more ways than binary to view narrative. There is no question that cultures of the past contained more than just men and women, male and female. Unfortunately, the record is murky on this fluidity and in many cases intentionally obfuscated, either at the time or by the bias of archaeologists and historians post hoc.

I need to acknowledge here and now that I see you nonbinary readers, and I know that there are more gender-inclusive ways to go about mythological analysis. I do not pretend to have that level of expertise, but if you do, I can't wait to read your book on this subject. Please write it?

As the ancient mythos I'll be referencing seem to deal mainly in binary terms, when analyzing these stories, I'll be doing the same thing. This does impose limits on complex comprehension. My aim is to impart a *basic* understanding, which hopefully you can run with, and manipulate, and extend beyond the initial binary scope of the translations and models we have to work from.

So, now, the terms.

SEX

Sex (or *biological sex*) refers to physiological categories that nominally define men and women. These theoretically meet an objective or scientific criteria (such as skeletal structure or genetics).

The vocabulary terms most anthropologists use when discussing *biological sex* are *female* and *male*.

As opposed to *gender*.

GENDER

Gender refers to cultural categories that are composed of *socially* constructed attributes, behaviors, roles, and activities. These are defined by what a given society considers appropriate for men and women (and, in several cases, third genders). In other words, there are social criteria for gender.

The vocabulary terms most anthropologists use when discussing *gender* are *feminine* and *masculine,* while acknowledging the fact that gender runs a spectrum between and sometimes outside of the two.

My pronoun use, when referring to a main character of a Heroine's Journey in the abstract, will be she/her, and when referring to the main character of a Hero's Journey, he/him. When using a specific example, I will use the pronouns of the example under discussion.

READ THIS BIT!

It's super important

Please understand that, while a character may present *biologically* as *male,* he may be gendered *feminine* by the overarching journey.

Harry Potter, for example, is a *heroine.*

And while a character may present *biologically* as *female,* she may be gendered *masculine* by her journey.

Wonder Woman (in the 2017 film by the same name) is a *hero.*

I'm going to put this another way, because, oh jeez, this is so flipping important.

A *female* presenting person can undertake a *Hero's Journey.*

A *male* presenting person can undertake a *Heroine's Journey.*

What does this mean?

Just because you are writing a woman as your main character doesn't mean you are automatically writing a Heroine's Journey.

> The *Heroine's Journey* is NOT simply the *Hero's Journey* undertaken by a woman.
>
> It's *narratively* different, not *biologically* different.

Joseph Campbell, the original propagator of analyzing the Hero's Journey, is reputed to have said:

> "Women don't need to make the journey. In the whole mythological journey, the woman is there. All she has to do is realize that she's the place people are trying to get to."

This quote was supposed to have been reported second-hand by Murdock, his student. I couldn't find corroborating evidence to support this, as Campbell never wrote this down. Reporting here: gailcarriger.com/HJ_quote (redirect to an online source).

Reddit questions whether it actually originated with Campbell here: gailcarriger.com/HJ_reddit (redirect to an online source)

Apocryphal or not, the statement is widely shared and discussed and is an interesting to examine closely.

1. It exposes the fact that psychoanalysis conflates gender and biological sex.
2. It implies that those undertaking a journey can only be men. It associates female individuals

(humans capable of their own journeys) with feminine archetypes as represented in the Hero's Journey.

3. It turns the female/feminine (remember, erroneously conflated) into location and place, while giving male/masculine the only access to personal autonomy: *He is the person on the journey while she's nothing more than the place he is trying to get to.*

There's a lot to unpack here. We'll come back to this statement a few more times during the course of this book, because it's actually really fun to tease out the nuances of its inaccuracies. I know, I'm a bit warped.

Right now, I'd like to use it mostly to illustrate the fact that things get awfully muddied when we conflate the biological sex of the main character with their narrative arc. They are *not* the same thing.

You see what I mean about semantics and terms?

GENDERED

To that end, in the context of this book, the term *gendered* has to do with the following:

Characters or story elements that behave (consciously or not) as *masculine* or *feminine* because of associated tropes, archetypes, or narrative role, regardless of *biological sex* and its socially accepted associations.

In other words, from a writer's perspective you may be writing a man, but when looked at through the lens of the Heroine's Journey, he may be fulfilling a feminine role.

Speaking of tropes and archetypes, next up is a quick review of some writing/literary terminology, and how I'll be using that in this book as well. I'm trying to provide a nice firm foundation here to limit misunderstanding as much as possible.

WRITING TERMS & TERMINOLOGY

AKA authorial semantic gymnastics

I did not present these alphabetically because knowing one definition will better allow you to understand others. So, they are presented logically. You know, because I just want to mess with you.

POV CHARACTER VERSUS MAIN CHARACTER

A POV character is the *point of view* character, essentially the person relaying the story to the audience. This is often, but not always, the same as the *main character*. How is it not? Well, in Sherlock Holmes, for example, Watson is the POV character, but the stories are about Holmes, who is the *main character*.

PLOT

The *plot* of a story is how its characters move through space and time physically, emotionally, and mentally. In other words: First this happens, and then this happens, and then this happens.

PACE

The *pace* is the heartbeat of the story in terms of action, reaction, length of scene or chapter, dialogue, humor, description, sentence structure, and point of view switches (if you have multiple POVs). It is made up of *structural* elements.

In other words: The plot is *what* you write, the pace is *how* you write it.

BEATS

Sometimes called *plot beats*, *beats* form the component parts of a story's structure. They are necessary to the basic outline of a plot's sequences, which are endemic to (and expected by the readers of) specific genres or heroic journeys. A beat is an event that will have impact on later events (or sets up expectations thereof, e.g., red herrings). These tend to be discoveries, revelations, or action points that influence the main character's journey.

ARCHETYPE

An *archetype* is a recurring character or idea that is actually a symbol or motif. Mostly, I will focus on *archetypes* as represented in characters. Some examples of *archetypes* are:

- seductive witch / sorceress
- old crone / evil witch
- innocent Eve / virgin sacrifice (beautiful cinnamon roll too good for this world, too pure)
- trickster guide
- wise mentor

- alpha masculine love interest

In discussion, reviews, and critical analysis, *archetypes* are often conflated with *tropes*.

I suggest thinking of *archetypes* as more singular and associated with one specific character. From a writer's perspective, *archetypes* are more likely to be *plot* devices, presented in single moments of story. For example: Our main character meets the wise mentor (say, Obi-Wan Kenobi), they impart knowledge, they act in a parental role, they die. The story moves on.

On the other hand, *tropes* are more likely to be supporting elements of the story arc, tied into an overarching *theme* or world-building motif. As such, they will reoccur again and again.

TROPE

A *trope* is a culturally shared concept that is imbued with social meaning that helps to create a predictable metaphor or outcome. *Tropes* tend to have a multiplicity to them that *archetypes* do not. Some examples of tropes are:

- innate specialness, hidden abilities
- Madonna/whore complex, Oedipus complex
- magical boarding school
- competitive love triangle
- mysterious prophecy or fated outcome

Any fiction that relies heavily on the Heroine's or the Hero's Journey is, by its very nature, *trope*-filled. All commercial genre fiction falls into this category. A thriller novel or gritty noir mystery is no more or less *trope*-reliant than a contemporary romance or young adult book (referred to henceforth as YA).

The use of the word *tropey* as a criticism of a book or movie is, therefore, deeply worrying. It buys into a general literary critique of genre fiction as being somehow lesser than (or unequal by comparison to) other forms of less commercially driven fiction. You better believe we will be talking more about this topic in **Chapter 6: The Heroine's Journey Gets Devalued**.

NARRATIVE ELEMENTS

When I say *narrative elements,* I mean a combination of *tropes* and *archetypes* that are emblematic of a mythological journey or piece of genre fiction.

THEME

The *theme* is the central topic or implication of a story (AKA its emotional resonance). You can access *theme* by asking yourself:

What is this story about?

Themes can often be summed up in a single word or concept phrase (e.g., self-discovery, love, betrayal, coming of age). *Themes* are exemplified through your character's actions, utterances, or thoughts. *Macbeth*, for example, has a *theme* of unchecked ambition, uses the *trope* of a fated outcome, and has the evil witch *archetype* at the beginning of the story.

MESSAGE

The *message* of a story is the agenda or purpose of the writer's narrative (AKA the cultural commentary of the journey). A *message* is essentially the overarching impression of authorial intent left at the end of a story. You can access *message* by asking yourself:

What is the author implying or advocating?

Messages are exemplified through narrator voice/tone, story arc, and (most important) outcome. *Messages* can be intentional or unintentional, but are always present in any narrative.

Read that again, please. You see, if you write fiction, you are conveying a message. If you read fiction, you are absorbing an author's message. Often more than one.

For example, what is *The Boy Who Cried Wolf* about? It's about a boy who yelled "Wolf!" when there were no wolves around, until no one believed him when an actual wolf showed up. The *theme* is one of lying as betrayal of trust, and the schadenfreude that results. The *message* is: Don't lie about being in danger, because then when you really are in danger, no one will help you.

Themes and how you apply them as a writer will confer *messages*. Application, use, manipulation, and gendered presentation of characters and *archetypes* will also convey *messages*. Choice and use of (not to mention twists on) *tropes* and outcomes of climax and conflict will also convey *messages*. The Heroine's Journey and the Hero's Journey certainly impart a series of fascinating *messages* to readers.

Messaging can be subconscious, subversive, manipulative, and incredibly powerful both in purpose and self-definition.

Your writing conveys a *message* (or *messages*) whether you realize it or not.

From a business perspective, as a career author, your *messages* do more to define your voice and brand than anything else you produce when writing. Certainly, you'll find yourself coming back to and exploring similar *narrative elements* and *themes*, but it's your *messages* that convey to readers a moral and ethical point of view – a core belief system, if you will. Your audience will unconsciously associate you, as a storyteller and as a person, with your *messages*.

As a reader, you may find yourself gravitating toward certain authors or certain genres and yet challenged to articulate why. I, for example, comfort-read gay romances. It wasn't until I began delving into the *messages* that I realized it is the concept of a loving found family, common in these books, that really attracts me to them. This is a message of support I find myself writing, originally accidentally. But it is one that has certainly become part of my brand, so that now I write it intentionally.

Righto, so these are the terms I'll be using throughout this book. Now, let's get on to the journeys themselves.

CHAPTER 3: HERO'S JOURNEY BEATS, THEMES & MESSAGES

Hero's Journey basic beats

I'm starting with the Hero's Journey. Why? Because the Hero's Journey exists heavily in the zeitgeist as a known entity. I can depend upon you, dear reader, to have at least a passing familiarity with this narrative. It seems to be something that most fiction writers know at least a little bit about.

I want to give you a solid touchstone before wandering into territories unknown. If you can understand how I analyze something familiar to you, then hopefully you will be able to understand how I analyze something unfamiliar.

Also, I am covering the Hero's Journey first because it will aid in our understanding of how the Heroine's Journey is different. I want to give you a foundation for comparison, and this is the best way to do that.

Without further ado... here is a "basic beats" outline of the Hero's Journey from a writer's perspective.

HERO'S JOURNEY BEATS

Our hero usually has a miraculous conception, semidivine birth, or inherited specialness.

Call to adventure

The hero refuses the call.

He receives aid from a mentor and/or the supernatural.

Withdrawal AKA Quest

The hero abandons his community and begins his quest.

He is tempted, distracted, and encounters many obstacles.

He visits the underworld (can be thought of as a second withdrawal, can be metaphorical).

He defeats his enemy one on one and retrieves a boon (sometimes the same thing).

Return

The hero is acknowledged for his success, presented with a reward, honored.

The hero receives glory but also isolation (pathos).

Check out a visual representation of the Hero's Journey here: gailcarriger.com/HJ_hero (redirect to a wikipedia article).

And now, let's talk about the themes underlying this journey.

THINGS TO NOTICE

Tracking patterns in the hero's narrative

The first things I would really love all storytellers to recognize in the Hero's Journey are repeated patterns of *withdrawal* and *return*. My breakdown above lists the basic beats, but the middle withdrawal section can, and often does, occur multiple times. Poor old Heracles had twelve of these withdrawals and returns (AKA labors) to undertake.

These patterns may be physical (in Greek mythology in particular), or they may be mental (common in a lot of tragedies), or they may be emotional (common in literary fiction). But the pattern always exists, and will usually be repeated over and over again.

The second thing that I hope all storytellers notice about the Hero's Journey, as I use it to analyze pop culture in the upcoming examples, is that *withdrawal* is an act the hero undertakes *voluntarily*. This withdrawal moves him away from civilization and/or civilized behavior. He chooses it and he engages in the pattern, usually in pursuit of something beyond his reach (the boon).

That boon can take many forms, including personhood or self-identity (see a lot of coming-of-age stories), but it is a symbol of (and a reward for) his victory. When you're writing a hero, he goes into motion of his own free will. His motivation is *very* different from that of a heroine.

Many talk about the Hero's Journey as a coming-of-age model – one of increased understanding of the world, separation from the safety of childhood and family, and development of solo personhood and self. To this end, a Hero's Journey is one of self-actualization and increased isolation, and the hero rises above obstacles and slays enemies and better understands himself.

The hero must, eventually, go it alone. He finds his strength from within in order to conquer his enemies.

As I review our pop-culture examples of the Hero's Journey, please keep these two things in mind:

1. This journey is a repeated pattern of withdrawal and return.
2. Those withdrawals are voluntary as increased isolation yields self-reliant strength.

Something to note, as I explore how to be an intentional author with regard to these narratives, is that my pop culture examples may not be equally intentional with their activation of these journeys.

I don't know what the writers of these books or scripts were thinking. Did they mean to use the Hero's Journey or the Heroine's? Perhaps they accessed them subconsciously.

My idea with these examples is to show you that it can, in fact, be intentional if you so wish.

HERO'S JOURNEY EXAMPLE 1

Wonder Woman

For my first model of the Hero's Journey in pop culture, I've chosen the Warner Brothers 2017 movie, *Wonder Woman*. It's remarkably accurate in conforming to a traditional Hero's Journey narrative, and yet it features a woman in the titular role. To understand this next section, it would be best for you to have seen this movie (as opposed to the comic books or TV show). If you haven't, you can go watch it. I'll wait. Or you can skip to my second example, which is the first original *Star Wars* movie.

Right, ready? Here we go.

Wonder Woman could not be a more classic example of the Hero's Journey. The fact that Diana, Princess of the Amazons, is biologically a woman doesn't make any difference whatsoever to this movie being a Hero's Journey.

First, we have a miraculous conception and divine birth. This ties right into Greek mythology. Diana is a demigod in truth, and fated to fight for glory, much in the same vein as most ancient Greek heroes like Achilles, Jason, or Heracles.

CALL TO ADVENTURE

Next comes Diana's call to adventure, in the form of a male intruder on her sacred island. She has already developed a mentor relationship, and that mentor is killed at the moment of the call. She engages in a classic initial refusal of the summons, after which she receives aid from the supernatural (in her case, a magic sword and other tools/weapons). The threat is revealed (a great war caused by Ares) and her quest is defined (find and stop/kill Ares).

WITHDRAWAL

Diana then undertakes her quest, voluntarily leaving the Amazon island. This is a symbolic (or in her case, literal) abandonment of family and community or civilization, toward the unknown and chaotic. In other words, she is undertaking great risk. Risk, for a hero, is an opportunity for personal growth, improved skills, and social dominance. And, in many cases, to fulfill their destiny.

The act of withdrawal is a voluntary sloughing off of the safety net, but it is also a rejection of the unchanging stasis of structured society that confines and limits the hero (the hearth and home, the strictures of domestic and political obligation). This withdrawal also incorporates abandonment of all parental figures and familial networks.

This move toward solitary action is the hero discovering their power.

The hero has now begun the quest and at this juncture is likely to face various temptations, distractions, and obstacles. One of the most common diversionary tactics is sex (or love or romance). The interesting thing about *Wonder Woman* is that the sexual seductress is a man. Steve acts the part of seducer, and despite the fact that he is assisting Diana on her quest, his Hero's Journey obligation is still to hold her back and stop her from completing her quest using his sexual powers. (Much as Circe does to Odysseus, Medea to Jason, and so forth.)

Diana then engages in her first descent into the underworld. The place she must cross as a warrior is called No Man's Land. She must cross this void alone, and the aid that is offered may be useful to her (but means great risk to those who offer) and usually distracts her as she worries about the safety of others.

During the quest that follows, there are additional moments of withdrawal, such as when Diana goes alone (with her sword at her back – literally) through the party. This is also an excellent example of one of the continued narrative elements of the Hero's Journey, in which crowds represent a threat to the hero.

At the climax, Diana battles the villain alone, one on one. This is the final descent, as Diana pursues Ludendorff (thinking he is Ares) to a base where deadly gas is loaded into aircraft. Ares reveals himself, they fight, and her love interest/friend engages in noble self-sacrifice. Diana kills Ares.

In Diana's case, her boon is partly nested in her fated destiny to defeat Ares, partly in coming into her full powers, and partly in the credence her victory over him gives her as a superhero – an acknowledged master of two worlds (human and immortal, mundane and supernatural). By the end of her withdrawal, Diana has lost much, and her reward is in defeat of her enemy and acknowledged victory over near impossible odds.

RETURN

Only after victory over her opponent can Diana return to civilization. But in classic hero fashion, her original civilization is no longer comfortable for her. She has outgrown it. She is pleased with the recognition and acknowledged mastery she has achieved, but the ending of the movie is, in a word, lonely. She no longer fits in back on the island of the Amazons. She knows too much of the outside world. She has grown beyond them, so she cannot go home, but she also does not entirely fit into the new world of modern humans, because of her origin and her superhero status.

Because she is a true hero, the final scene in the movie makes it abundantly clear that Diana is solitary – the last scene depicts a future in which she is looking at a photo of her dead companions, alone in her office. She is remembering her glory while being shown as consigned to isolation by her very nature.

This is a hallmark of a Hero's Journey: that the ending be steeped in bittersweet pathos and that the outcome is a solitary one for the hero.

It behooves me to mention at this juncture that another way to know you're experiencing a Hero's Journey in pop culture is when depictions of power occur in isolation. If you think back to enduring imagery from this movie, not to mention the posters used to advertise it, Diana is almost always pictured alone when she is at her most powerful.

When you write a hero, isolate him to show him in control and in power.

3

HERO'S JOURNEY EXAMPLE 2

Star Wars: Episode IV A New Hope

I need hardly say that the first *Star Wars* movie is a Hero's Journey. Both George Lucas (the creator of *Star Wars*) and Joseph Campbell (the creator of the Hero's Journey as a field of study) openly acknowledge the correlation. Lucas admits to having read *The Hero with a Thousand Faces* (1949) and intentionally using it as a template for *Star Wars* (documented via quotations from Lucas in the authorized biography *Joseph Campbell: A Fire in the Mind* by Stephen and Robin Larsen, 2002, p. 541).

So, here we go!

Luke's birth contains elements of his being fated or ordained for something heroic (although we don't necessarily know about this in the first movie). We sure do learn about it as things proceed.

CALL TO ADVENTURE

Luke follows some droids and encounters a mentor in the guise of Obi-Wan Kenobi, and supernatural aid in the form of a lightsaber. Obi-Wan urges Luke to seek his destiny and learn the ways of the Force. Luke tries to go home, at which juncture it's made clear this is no longer an option. His family is taken away from him, his parental figures murdered, and his home burned. Even at the beginning of his quest, this hero can never truly return home.

WITHDRAWAL

Luke then begins his quest. In his first major withdrawal (he will engage in this pattern a lot through the course of these movies), Luke abandons what is left of his family and community. Princess Leia Organa shows up to act the required role of seductress and distraction.

Luke engages in a virtual descent into the underworld (the garbage masher). His mentor/father figure is killed, finally leading us to the point where Luke, alone in his fighter, takes on the insurmountable odds of a whole Death Star.

He defeats the enemy and retrieves a boon, which again takes the form of acknowledged mastery and recognition of his skills.

RETURN

The movie ends with a classic return motif, the ritual presentation of medals of honor, a physical manifestation of recognition of victory. Interestingly enough, the final scene is one of glory within the group, unusual in a Hero's

Journey, and perhaps tied to the humor and heist trope component of these movies.

All three of the original *Star Wars* movies do this – end on a pan-out group shot which generally is more common to the Heroine's Journey in film.

4

ADDITIONAL EXAMPLES OF THE HERO

Just a few more so you have a range of comparison

The Hero's Journey shows up on screen in such movies as *Die Hard* (1998); the James Bond franchise; and *Deadpool* (2016). In fact, most solitary superhero movies and origin stories are the Hero's Journey; see *Spider-Man: Into the Spider-Verse* (2018).

Although honestly, don't ask me about *Black Panther* (2018) because I have puzzled over it in detail and it has pretty compelling elements of both journeys as well as capers, so I'm stumped. I talk more about this in the **References** section.

On the page, you can find it in the Jack Reacher (1997) books (and anything in that suspense wheelhouse), noir and crime thrillers, some science fiction and fantasy (SF/F), particularly those with quest or paladin tropes, and some YA (like *The Divergent Series*, 2011–2013).

HERO'S JOURNEY HIDDEN MESSAGES

There are some enduring narrative elements and messages in the Hero's Journey that I think are important for writers to recognize. Especially when we are about to delve deeply into the Heroine's Journey.

HOW THE HERO'S JOURNEY VIEWS FEMININITY

Feminine characters (be they gods, foils, or love interests) thwart the hero via stagnation and/or distraction. Witches (goddesses, sorceresses) when present (symbolically or otherwise) usually represent chaotic forces of nature, or civilizing forces of structure, who are attempting to stop the hero with sex or marriage or death (sometimes all three). A hero like Odysseus experiences all these elements over and over and over again.

To that end, wives or daughters (even good ones like Penelope) represent civilization, which is not a positive thing for our hero.

Why?

Because civilization seeks to control the hero through inertia, and inertia is the hero's ultimate enemy. If he cannot move through space and time, he cannot accomplish his quest. Feminine characters seek to pause the hero's momentum.

A hero's quest is his whole purpose within the narrative. Attaining success, vanquishing his enemy, retrieving the boon, and enjoying the accompanying glory and acknowledgment all define him and his identity. The feminine interjected characters, therefore, subvert his very identity.

HOW THE HERO'S JOURNEY VIEWS SUCCESS

Thus it behooves storytellers to consider the nature of success, how our main character defines success for himself, and how we define it for him on the page.

The definition of success is a key difference between the Hero's and the Heroine's Journeys.

A hero succeeds by voluntarily withdrawing himself from his culture, family, and the world of social interactions. Our hero succeeds by going it alone; for him, *isolation leads to victory*.

Which is not to say that he can't have any family or friends or lovers in his story. Sometimes a family member or lover is the boon to be won at the end (although this causes the familial member to be objectified and lose personhood under the strictures of the Hero's Journey). It's also likely that a family member (often an uncle) is the bad guy (waves at Horus versus Set or *Spider-Man: Into the Spider-Verse* 2018).

Also, the death of the father/mentor figure is often the inciting event that drives the hero into violence, anger, and action.

Now perhaps we can understand a little more of the background behind this statement:

> "In the whole mythological journey, the woman is there. All she has to do is realize that she's the place people are trying to get to."

The *whole mythological journey* only takes into account the Hero's Journey. The *woman who is there* is actually not a biological woman at all but a feminine archetype as required by this kind of journey (and this kind of journey *alone*). This statement conflates notions of *place* with the *purpose* of the Hero's Journey (his boon) even as it conflates *people* with the hero himself.

In your story, for example, if a hypothetical girlfriend is nothing more than a reward for a hero's job well done, this is profoundly different from her being an active network of help, communication, and cohesion.

For the heroine, a hypothetical girlfriend is there on the journey *with* her. For the hero, his girlfriend is most likely a plot device to spur him into greater solitary action (check out the concept of *fridging* for classic examples of this).

This nuanced difference ties to the notions of success and achievement, which are profoundly different between these two journeys. Oh yes, we are so coming back to this. I promise.

HOW THE HERO'S JOURNEY VIEWS STRENGTH

Most significant to those of us interested in the Heroine's Journey is that for a hero in a Hero's Journey, a prevailing concept and perpetuated message is that *asking for (or needing) help is BAD*.

Because a hero who asks for help is perceived as weak by the story – remember, his goals and victory are invested in conquest and solo achievement – a hero who asks for help will be perceived as weak by the audience as well. To that end, depictions of the hero as powerful and in his greatest moments of strength and personal growth will inevitably occur in *isolation*.

Since the hero requires separation to achieve his goals, all attachment threatens his success. No matter how much he may love his wife, that wife represents risk through which the hero may be pressured away from his quest. The heroine, we will find, is the opposite.

For the hero, *sharing* (particularly sharing power or glory) weakens the boundaries of self, which gives new meaning to the concept of *selfless acts*. Such acts diminish the hero, and make less of him (or in the case of a tragic hero, bring about his demise).

He who portions out achievement loses parts of his own identity. This is not the same as portioning out his boon, or sharing the physical representation of his victory, like a medal or a healing herb.

The Heroine's Journey, on the other hand, explores the notion that giving away something of oneself and sharing achievement can actually contribute to the evolution of both characters, thus enriching the heroine's life and everyone's prospective success.

HOW THE HERO'S JOURNEY VIEWS VICTORY

For the hero, *victory* is in destroying his enemies, dealing out death, enacting his revenge, and taking retribution. He will usually end up alone. If he does *get the girl*, he probably can't keep her for long. Think of characters like James Bond or Jack Reacher and other classic heroes in the thriller genre.

In *Wonder Woman*, Diana gets Steve, but then must watch him sacrifice himself. Even if the love interest lasts the whole story, a sympathetic feminine character (be it lover, friend, or foil) will be killed or in some other manner turned into a plot device to motivate the hero in the next scene, book, or movie.

There's another complex repercussion to the concepts of power, victory, and success as they are presented by the Hero's Journey. There is a tacit glorification of violence (which is connected to isolation and victory) combined with a suspicion of sex and romantic relationships (because they represent both connection and the seductive nature of the feminine).

We can see how this percolates into the zeitgeist in terms of social censorship, genre worthiness, and culture-wide value judgments – movie ratings, for example. When governments and critics get involved and unconsciously apply superiority and preferential treatment to the Hero's Journey, they're unconsciously endorsing that journey's themes and messages.

HOW THE HERO'S JOURNEY VIEWS SACRIFICE

On a more authorial note, a quick word on self-sacrifice. If or when our hero attempts to save the world (and not just take revenge and defeat his enemy) or sacrifices himself for the good of others, the hero will usually die in the attempt.

A noble yet tragic Hero's Journey is relatively common.

This is opposed to the heroine, who usually manages compromise for the good of mankind (and not to die). Although – give her a chance – a heroine can also have a heart-wrenchingly tragic ending, which we will talk about more in the context of the Heroine's Journey themes.

Just mentioning this, you know, in case you want to make your readers cry.

REVIEW: HERO'S JOURNEY NARRATIVE STRUCTURE

Quick recap and preparation to use the Hero's Journey as a basis for comparison

Something you'll find I come back to again and again with both heroic narratives is the fact that these journeys are *guides* to storytelling. They are not step-by-step outlines that you (or anyone else) should follow exactly, nor do they need to be followed in order.

Nor are all elements guaranteed to be present in every single movie or book of a corresponding type.

You'll find yourself starting to notice the signal markers of the Hero's Journey versus the Heroine's Journey a great deal more after reading this book (or I hope you will), but that doesn't mean every pop culture thing you encounter out in the world can (or should) conform to one journey or the other.

In other words, please don't get obsessed with trying to fit everything into neat little binaries.

These narratives have changed and evolved over the years – sometimes in rather insidious ways. Particularly in commercial genre fiction, both journeys have been profoundly impacted by the archetypes and tropes of the Gothic literary movement (see **Chapter 7**).

Other variations have popped up as well, combining the two journeys or injecting heroines into hero narratives and vice versa. Some examples include the buddy cop dynamic; capers, heists, and group quests; the use of multiple POVs; and the presence of character foils. All of these further muddy the waters of forcing the story to fit exactly into one journey or the other. **Chapter 8** delves deeply into some of the complex interweaving we writers can do with these journeys.

I'm hoping to help you recognize patterns, beats, themes, and messages. Please do not feel you must force your story to conform to one narrative or another. If it doesn't want to go in one direction, it's probably trying to tell you something.

All that said, I'm acknowledging here and now that many stories *do*, in fact, conform, and there is nothing at all wrong with that either.

> A story can be the Hero's Journey, but not have to hit every note of that journey.

Humans like to think in terms of black and white. Our narratives, however, are more flexible than that.

What I'm trying to do here is twofold:

1. First, I want to train you to recognize these journeys when they *do* appear, whatever their form, so that your pattern recognition instincts are honed and your brain trained to tell stories.
2. Second, I want to give you two complete

toolboxes to draw from, for so long we have been working from just the one.

As storytellers, I hope this helps you pick up and use whatever aspects speak to you. These narrative elements are tools of clarity, like the rules of grammar, and similarly it's best to know the rules before you break them. Like grammar, if unconsciously or casually misapplied, readers will feel at best confused, and at worst betrayed.

Once again, the basic outline of the Hero's Journey is:

HERO'S JOURNEY BEATS

Call to adventure

Refusal

Aid

Withdrawal AKA Quest

Abandon community

Visit underworld

Retrieve reward

Return

Recognition

Glory & isolation

Please do remember:

1. This journey is a repeated pattern of withdrawal and return, and those withdrawals are voluntary.

2. Victory is in isolation and asking for help is bad.

Now, let's move on to the foundational myths of the Heroine's Journey, which will help us understand the themes and narrative elements necessary when writing that narrative.

CHAPTER 4: BASIC STRUCTURE & FOUNDATIONAL MYTHS

A mythological foundation for the Heroine's Journey

Why do we need to know these ancient myths? Because so many of our most popular modern stories are sourced in ancient mythology, and rely on these patterns to be successful. And because the heartbeat of narrative in the western world leans on the Heroine's Journey.

I've chosen three Heroine's Journey myths to help provide a foundational understanding of this core narrative. The three main characters are also all goddesses: Demeter, Isis, and Inanna.

WHY THESE THREE?

Well, they are the ones with whom I am most comfortable and familiar. I like them, I've analyzed them a lot, and I think they demonstrate the key narrative elements of the

Heroine's Journey that make it unique. This is not to say these are the only ones. In fact, I'm hoping to see a spate of resurrected myths coming to the fore, highlighting the complex nature and scope of this narrative.

I am telling these three myths my way, because this is my interpretation. They are different from each other, but they do share some important similarities. For one thing, the main character is female and a full goddess (no demigods here).

WHY ARE THEY GODDESSES?

There are very few female heroines of the demigod type in Greek mythology (and before you throw Atalanta at me, she's a hero, not a heroine). It's my opinion that goddesses, being super powerful and representing natural elements, are the only model of females in power that can be permitted by a patriarchal society in an active, autonomous role.

There is something about goddesses being both people and divine symbols that permits functional autonomy and allows them to become a narrative myth and undertake their own journey.

WHY IS THIS NECESSARY?

That's a whole other book.

It's the story behind these myths that conveys a *message* that women in power are intrinsically dangerous as a concept, and in myth. These are the kinds of concepts your own story can convey, or work to undermine. As you look at these myths, keep in mind the messages they relay, and how you might activate them yourselves to encourage emotional resonances and empathy with an audience.

What our Heroine's Journey defines as strength, power, and success is diametrically opposed to the way these concepts are viewed in a Hero's Journey, and it is so much fun to play with.

So now, on to the really useful stuff. As I retell these three myths, here are the narrative beats of the Heroine's Journey that I encourage you to look out for:

HEROINE'S JOURNEY BASIC BEATS

The Descent (loss or separation)

Familial network is broken.

Pleas are ignored, resulting in an abdication of power.

Withdrawal is *involuntary*.

Family offers aid but no solution.

Result is isolation and danger.

The Search (forced withdrawal on a search for unity)

Loss of family means risk.

Disguise/subversion.

Appeal to surrogate family/network and an attempt to rebuild community.

Visit underworld.

Friends/family render aid.

The Ascent (or the return)

Negotiation for reunification results in a compromise benefiting all.

Network is established (or re-established in an altered form).

Revenge is irrelevant, glory is irrelevant.

The Heroine's Journey is one of building teams, creating cohesions, forming social relationships, ensuring civilization and posterity.

It also seeks balance and compromise.

I'll come back to (and explain further) these beats and the associated narrative elements and messages while analyzing and presenting the myths and two pop culture examples of the Heroine's Journey.

INTRODUCING THE MYTH OF DEMETER

Also called the Theft (or Rape) of Persephone

I'm basing my analysis of the Myth of Demeter on the *Homeric Hymn to Demeter* translated by Gregory Nagy (no date given, the translation seems to have been intentionally made public online by the author in conjunction with Harvard University - see redirect gailcarriger.com/HJ_Nagy). This is one of the more widely known and studied translations. I lean on it as the primary source, although there are, of course, variations throughout the ancient world and the translated history of the piece.

Demeter is a complicated goddess, probably the result of an incorporation of several localized harvest (agriculture) and fertility goddesses stretching back to the Mycenean period, if not earlier (Burkert 1985, 285). She was further adopted and subsequently bastardized by the Romans as Ceres. There developed a pretty thriving cult around Demeter (see the Eleusinian Mysteries) including a festival/pilgrimage based on this myth during both Greek and Roman times that further impacted this narrative, in a kind of mythological version of the game Telephone.

In other words, there are a lot of different versions of Demeter's Heroine's Journey out there from different times and places. I had to pick something, so I picked Homer and Nagy.

I came to Demeter late.

As a kid, my favorite Greek goddesses were always Athena and Artemis. Then, as I grew up, Athena's single-minded devotion to Zeus and her warlike nature and Artemis's obsession with purity and her vindictiveness began to trouble me. Not to mention their respective origin stories – I mean to say, the fact that Athena, goddess of wisdom, is literally born out of Zeus's head... this is, erm, worrying.

So then I began to feel an affinity for Hestia, oft neglected, quietly content goddess of the hearth. It should come as no surprise to anyone reading this that I am *not* a quiet person, so it was rather as a last resort that I eventually ended up learning, loving, and identifying with Demeter and her fiery hunt for her lost daughter (literally, she carries torches in most depictions of her search). Although, to be perfectly honest, Hermes has my heart and always will. Gotta love a trickster god.

Where was I?

Oh yeah... Demeter!

2

DEMETER'S STORY

No one steals my daughter from me, not even the god of death!

DEMETER'S DESCENT

Demeter is in possession of power. She is a queen on a throne on Mount Olympus, where she presides over her domain as goddess of the harvest, food, agriculture, fertility, seasons, and the cycle of life. She wears a crown (headdress) symbolizing her power and dominion over mankind.

Her daughter, the fair maiden Persephone, is wandering around picking flowers in a field while Demeter is doing something else. The earth opens up in a great chasm. Hades appears and abducts Persephone, taking her down to the underworld.

Demeter does not know what has happened to her daughter. She only knows that her child is missing and that Persephone would never leave of her own free will. Persephone must have been taken.

When none of the other gods will tell Demeter what happened, she abdicates her throne on Mount Olympus. The symbolism of this is very cool – she rips off her head-dress (crown) and casts it aside in anger.

This is a classic marker of most Heroine's Journeys – the rejection of divine power (or defined social role) as a result of a familial connection being taken or severed. A key moment in any Heroine's Journey is that precipitating fracture of family that will drive her into action.

Another way to read this is as Demeter tearing off her veil – a demonstration of loss of chastity and innocence. This is a voluntary awakening that could have sexual connotations, and often will, in your YA or romance novel.

DEMETER'S SEARCH

Since Demeter's only recourse seems to be to find Persephone herself, the goddess leaves Olympus to search for her daughter. She withdraws from the safety of civilization. In Demeter's case, this is her Olympian throne and literal seat of divine power. She simultaneously abandons markers of queenly divinity (like the headdress), sacrificing elements of her own identity in order to get her daughter back.

Demeter searches in vain, alone, and as she searches, civilization suffers (there is a terrible famine). During her search, Demeter is usually depicted crownless and, holding a blazing torch, she wanders the earth.

Hecate, Demeter's sister goddess, comes to her, offering up information. This is our first example of the kind of networking that a heroine requires to complete her quest. Hecate says that she heard something but that she didn't actually see anything, and perhaps they should talk to one of the other gods. Hecate is the goddess of magic, witchcraft, the night, moon, ghosts, and necromancy.

Together (and that is a key word here), Demeter and Hecate find and persuade Helios (the god of the sun who would have seen everything from his chariot in the heavens) to tell them the truth of Persephone's abduction. He does so reluctantly, but also advises Demeter to accept the separation with grace as Hades would make for a powerful son-in-law.

Demeter now knows that Hades took her daughter, and that the other gods (if Helios is any indication) will not help her to get Persephone back. As a result, she emotionally withdraws. She wallows in her a grief even worse than before.

Why is it even worse now? Because Helios's reluctance to help represents another severing of her familial network. Demeter cannot appeal to the gods (her brothers), because they will not face Hades on her behalf.

So Demeter disguises herself as an old crone and wanders the earth, continuing to punish the world with famine. At this juncture, she has abdicated her rights as goddess and queen, and even her beauty and the power it represents. This is, essentially, a complete identity withdrawal. Demeter has given up every characteristic she held formerly as acts of personhood. It's also a common marker of the Heroine's Journey – the element of disguise and of shifting identity in pursuit of reunification.

Eventually on her wanderings, Demeter the crone is discovered by the daughters of King Keleos and Queen Metaneira, and taken in by them to become a nurse (or nanny) to the baby prince of their household. This is another great marker of the Heroine's Journey: found or second family, and the constant need to further a relationship network. Still, Demeter remains depressed. She sits on a low stool near the fire, speaking to no one, and dwelling in sadness.

Demeter's depression is only alleviated by Iambe, Goddess of raunchy humor, who comes before her and makes jokes. Demeter actually laughs and her mood is improved greatly.

Iambe is the personification of iambic tradition; she provokes laughter and fertility, and the jokes she's telling Demeter are probably pretty darned obscene. However, we must remember that Demeter is also a fertility goddess. (If you want something interesting, look up the statuary of Iambe.)

I mention Iambe because another marker of the Heroine's Journey is humor. Comedy is something very easy for writers to inject into this particular narrative and it's also a great tool for pacing. Levity is healing for a heroine. In the Hero's Journey, humor can be used, but more often it's a distraction.

Demeter, still needing to establish familial networking, decides to turn the young prince (her charge) into an immortal (thus conferring her own divinity upon him and making him more her child). She does this by burning the mortality out of him, literally, resting him in the fire as if he were a log or wood. Unfortunately, his mother, the queen, catches Demeter at this, and rushes in screaming to rescue the prince.

Chaos ensues, Demeter drops the baby, the sisters come in and start clucking over him, and Demeter throws off her crone disguise and reveals herself as the beautiful goddess she is. (And if you're thinking there's a whole lesson here in hospitality, and being nice to strangers because they may be gods in disguise, sure thing.)

The queen and king prostrate themselves before Demeter and beg her mercy. As recompense, she demands that King Keleos build her a beautiful massive temple. This is key, because a big building with religious purpose is one of the single best visual and concrete examples of civilization. What does a heroine ask for when she has been wronged? A key representation of civilization – a monument to organized religion. What would a hero do? Probably chop off everyone's heads. But I digress.

There is also an indication that Demeter, at this juncture, takes pity on starving mankind and teaches a young man, possibly another prince, the secrets of agriculture (but this is not clear in Nagy's translation).

Demeter assumes the throne in her new temple and, one by one, the other gods come down from Olympus and beg her for clemency. She refuses, saying that she will never return to Olympus, never take up her thrown or divine duties, and never allow a harvest to be reaped until she sees her daughter again.

DEMETER'S ASCENT

Realizing that Demeter is very near to destroying all of humanity (and then who would worship him?), Zeus sends Hermes to the underworld to bring Persephone back.

Persephone ascends up to earth, and she and her mother are gloriously reunited. Unfortunately, Hades gave her some pomegranate seeds to eat, which bind Persephone to spend a third of every year with Hades as his wife in the underworld. She's spend the other two thirds with her mother on Mount Olympus.

This is the final important beat in a Heroine's Journey: *compromise*.

Our heroine is good at compromise (therein lies the power of connection) and it's a good thing for everyone that she is. Because the heroine's ability to negotiate for a compromise results in an integration of power, and a positive impact on the world and civilization.

Balance is key here. In the case of this myth, Demeter has taught mankind agriculture and also arranged the seasons. She has won no boon and taken no revenge; in fact, she has turned her trials into a benefit for all mankind – the seasons and a steady food supply.

③

INTRODUCING THE MYTH OF ISIS

Also called the Resurrection of Osiris

Actually, *The Resurrection of Osiris* is what this myth is most often called in the historical record (Roman) and the western mindset (turn of the last century French and English). You can take a look at the citations at the back of this book for this myth if you like wincing a lot.

If you're thinking:

> "Wait a minute. The story of a major, powerful goddess questing all over Egypt to collect her husband's body parts (with her sister's help), build temples, conceive and rear a new king-god, and bring about the afterlife and idea of continuation of humanity is *named after her dead husband?*"

Yeah, I am so with you. My eyebrow is most certainly *raised*.

The primary source materials for the myth of Isis are scattered and filtered through the lenses of ensuing ancient cultures, not to mention the Victorians. I chose to rely on two major researchers of the Isis myth: Budge (1895, 1911 and 1960) and Shaw (2014). See the full citations at the back of this book.

In turn, these gentlemen are relying on a compilation of cobbled-together sources. They both reference ancient Greek writers who recorded the Osiris myth: Plutarch's *De Iside et Osiride and Moralia. Vol. v: Isis and Osiris* (1936 translation), and Diodorus Siculus's *Library of History* (1933 translation). These two ancient gentlemen tend to reinterpret the Isis myth through the lens of, unsurprisingly, their own goddess, Demeter.

The Isis myth was directly sourced by Budge and Shaw in the following three archaeological fragments, commonly translated into English as: *The Account in the Pyramid Texts*; *Papyrus Salt 825;* and *The Lamentations of Isis and Nephthys* (available online as a translation of *Berlin Papyrus 3008* dating to the Ptolemaic Dynasty 323–30 BCE).

Despite this desperate patchwork of creation, the myth of Isis is probably my favorite myth of all time.

It is, however, challenging for the western mind to fully comprehend. The ancient Egyptians were rather flexible in their application of roles and function to gods and mythology. They had, for example, multiple different creation myths that all comfortably coexisted, not to mention various different notions of the soul and where it went in the afterlife.

There is a multiplicity to Egyptian mythology, to the definition of gods themselves (and their many hats and heads) which means they do not always fit comfortably into domains, boxes, descriptions, physical identities, or symbols. One goddess can be, and is, many things at once.

The ancient Egyptian civilization also existed for three thousand years (or so). During this extensive period, the myth of Isis changed and morphed into various iterations. I must beg you to forgive my summation and preferred retelling (it's no doubt rather simplistic) and urge you to track down and read the originals if you can.

Meanwhile, read on, because the myth of Isis has much to delight! In the following pages, you'll encounter a missing phallus, sister solidarity, and mummy resurrection.

Come on, what's not to love?

ISIS'S STORY

Cut my husband into pieces, will you?

There are various ways this myth begins. In some iterations, Isis is married to Set and cheats on him with Osiris,
while her sister (and sometimes identical twin) Nephthys
is married to Osiris. In most, Isis is married to Osiris
when Set launches a bid to take over the throne and rule
the known world. In many versions, Nephthys, Isis's
sister/sister wife, has a child with Osiris. This child is
Anubis, whom Isis then adopts. (Adoption was very
common in ancient Egypt.)

There are many iterations because we have many sources.
Because the ancient Egyptians existed for such a long
time, myths evolved differently in different parts of the
same empire. Just think of this is as a vast game of
communication where not everything is written down,
very few can read anyway, and even if they could, everyone
tells it differently.

ISIS'S DESCENT

Set, god of chaos, conspires to kill his brother Osiris, ruler of the gods and ends up trapping Osiris's body in a tree (Budge 1960, 54). With her husband/brother/lover familial network broken, Isis abdicates her goddess power and queenship. She engages in the descent, disguises herself, and eventually manages to rescue Osiris (or at least liberate his body).

Unfortunately, she then gets distracted (we aren't sure how) and Set manages to steal back Osiris's body.

Set cuts Osiris into 14 pieces (or 26 in some versions, but I learned it as 14 so I'm going with that). Set then scatters these pieces of Osiris all over the Nile river valley.

ISIS'S SEARCH

Isis begins hunting all over Egypt, gathering up all the different parts of Osiris. Sometimes she does this alone, but more often she is in the company of Nephthys (her sister) or dog-headed Anubis (her nephew/adopted son) and god of life to death transitions (among other things).

Because who best helps a heroine on her quest? Friends and family members. Nephthys in particular is devoted and adoring, helping Isis in any that she can, attempting to share the burden of the quest and the emotional loss of Osiris.

Isis is modestly successful on her search as she finds one body part after another. Nephthys and Anubis help Isis find the limbs of Osiris and give each one a proper burial. In some cases, she's reputed to have made little Osiris-body-part votives to bury instead of the actual body part, so she can keep all of Osiris's bits together for later. Each time Isis finds a piece of Osiris, she has a temple built (Budge 1911, Loc 2179) on that spot.

Demeter only got one temple, watch Isis get thirteen! Once again, these temples represent civilization (organized religion), and for a heroine this is no threat, as it would be for a hero.

Why only thirteen? Well, Isis can't find the fourteenth piece of Osiris.

Crisis! His phallus is missing. Oh no! Apparently, it was eaten by a fish (Shaw 2014, 74). (Well, we've all been there, right?)

So Isis does what she can, fashioning a fake phallus, and procreating with that in order to conceive an heir, Horus. Then she wraps up all the pieces of Osiris together and with the help of Nephthys and Anubis (god of mummification), they resurrect Osiris.

Often called the *Lamentations of Isis and Nephthys*, the two sisters call Osiris back into his body to live again (effectively creating the afterlife). I'm emphasizing the euphemistic bit in the passage quoted below, because I'm wildly amused by Budge trying to be all stiff and proper and circumspect.

> "She sought him untiringly, she wandered round and round about this earth in sorrow, and she alighted not without finding him. She made light with her feathers, she created air with her wings, and she uttered the death wail for her brother. *She raised up the inactive members of him whose heart was still, she drew from him his essence, she made an heir, she reared the child in loneliness,* and the place where he

was not known, and he grew in strength and stature, and his hand was mighty in the House of Keb."

— BUDGE 1895

Emphasis is mine (of course) because *drew from him his essence* indeed! Ha!

Anyhoo, Horus is raised by both Isis and Nephthys (Budge 1911 Loc 2524). He grows up, flaps off on his own heroic journey, defeats his uncle Set, takes over rulership of Upper and Lower Egypt, and all is well.

In some accounts, Isis goes through this whole cycle again with Horus, whom Set kills with a scorpion but who is resurrected by Thoth at the behest of Nephthys (Budge 1911). In some versions it is Anubis, not Horus, who tricks and kills Set.

Horus's story is a Hero's Journey of conquering the enemy. Isis, unsurprisingly, is uninterested in the revenge, victory, defeat side of the equation because she's got Heroine's Journey things to accomplish. So, she lets her son do his thing.

ISIS'S ASCENT

Horus takes over rulership on earth, Isis (with her sister and Anubis) has now created the afterlife for Osiris to rule over, and invented mummification so humans may have the afterlife themselves and continue to worship there.

Isis is then able to split her time (and to a certain extent, her identity) between living in Egypt (the Two Lands) with Horus and in the afterlife (which essentially mimics of the world above) with Osiris. She is often depicted next to either god; she may also be, portray, or stand behind the throne of rulership.

This is her compromise: not only partnership and the afterlife, but also a cyclical continuation that ties to the most core Egyptian beliefs – that this life continues in the next, and that the gods remain in power, regardless.

Isis might be my favorite Heroine's Journey.

I mean, she literally collects the pieces of her man and puts him back together again. It's such a fantastic representation of networking. Not to mention the constant presence and aid of her sister, Nephthys, who by some standards really didn't owe Isis anything.

Isis is strong in her friendships. She is powerful in her ability to literally put a god back together again. I hope you can see how this might translate to your own written words.

The amazing emotional resonance and appeal of many romances rests in this kind of cohesive push – particularly those where a good girl saves a bad boy (and if you're thinking of *Fifty Shades of Grey*, so am I). And yes, there is possible societal damage as a result of this concept, but you cannot deny, as writers or readers, that it is a powerfully *effective* story.

INTRODUCING THE MYTH OF INANNA

Also called The Descent of Ishtar

The Descent of Inanna was entirely unknown to me until I first studied it as an undergraduate. I was already very familiar with Isis and Demeter, but Inanna came to me later in life.

Inanna (in Sumerian) or Ishtar (in Assyrian) is the goddess of love, war, and sex (among other things). She is a much more violent goddess than Demeter or Isis and is often depicted with wings and multiple swords, having bird feet, and standing atop the backs of lions.

I'm basing my analysis of this myth on *Inanna: Queen of Heaven and Earth* by Diane Wolkstein and Samuel Noah Kramer (1993). This book is a compilation of translations from multiple scholars representing thirty different tablets and fragments, conducted from 1889 to 1963.

There are missing fragments and some segments are still open to interpretation. This is an archaeological record we are talking about here, collected during a time when scientific strictures were a great deal less rigorous, and objectivity wasn't even considered. It's more complicated than I have time to fully explore here. I recommend reading the original translation if you're particularly interested in Inanna. If you choose to do so, the source material is quite repetitive and song-like.

I have to admit that I don't like Inanna very much. She strikes me as probably a pretty unpleasant person.

You could clearly go out drinking with Demeter or Isis and have a great time. You know, chat about dismemberment and pomegranate allergies over a cider or two.

Inanna might be fun for a little while, but she'd probably start a bar fight, and you know she's one of *those* friends, full of complaints and a champion whiner, but great for gossip.

Also, a quick note to add that in one of her other myth fragments, *The Huluppu-Tree*, Inanna crosses paths with and activates the hero Gilgamesh when her sacred tree is occupied by a serpent and misbehaving. After asking her brother Utu, the valiant warrior, for help in ridding her tree of its unwelcome infestation, and being denied, Inanna goes to Gilgamesh, the hero of Uruk.

Gilgamesh puts on his armor, lifts his ax, and goes into Inanna's holy garden to defeat her enemy the serpent, splits her tree, and makes her a throne. In return, Inanna fashions for him symbols of power, called the *pukku* and *mikku*. (Wolkstein and Kramer, 8–9)

I mention this because I find it amusing to see Gilgamesh show up and assist Inanna when he holds such significance for denizens of the Hero's Journey.

I'll be addressing what happens when a hero (on a Hero's Journey) appears within the narrative structure of a Heroine's Journey in **Chapter 8**.

But first, let's discuss the complexity of the Inanna myth.

INANNA'S STORY

Love is a complicated matter of sisters, arranged marriages, and flies in bars

Inanna attempts to rule all planes of existence. It is not enough to be queen of heaven and earth; she wishes to rule the underworld as well. So, she vows to visit and win over Eriskigal, goddess of death.

This is perhaps an unusual start to a Heroine's Journey, as heroines are not normally motivated by a hunt for power, but she does hit many of the other key beats. (And this is probably the point where I remind you that just as every hero does not always take on *every* point in the Hero's Journey, so it is true with the heroine.)

INANNA'S DESCENT

In her first act of descent, Inanna abandons her place of power (heaven and earth) and her position as priestess to descend to the underworld (Wolkstein & Kramer 1993, 52). In most Heroine's Journeys, a visit to the underworld (metaphorical or actual) happens in the Search. Inanna is a bit hasty and the early appearance of this beat has to do with the fact that the severing of the family connection happens later, so the two are swapped.

Inanna's initial withdrawal is comparable to Demeter pulling off her crown and casting it aside. As with Demeter, there is a spatial aspect to Inanna's decent, as it mimics the idea of a downward spiral, under the earth, and lower than Inanna's seat of rulership and power (which is the tree throne).

Inanna approaches the underworld, accompanied by her faithful servant, Ninshubur. An interesting character, Ninshubur is primarily defined by her loyalty to Inanna and it's unclear whether she is bonded slave, free servant, true friend, or lover. In a behavioral context, one can think of her as almost sisterly, especially when compared to a later brother/sister relationship (between Inanna's husband and his sister) that will be highlighted in the resurrection section of the myth.

Regardless, Inanna instructs Ninshubur to request aid of the gods, should Inanna fail in her crusade to conquer death and achieve resurrection. Her servant agrees and waits faithfully at the entrance to the underworld for Inanna's return.

Eriskigal, goddess of death, allows Inanna to journey farther into her domain, but insists that at each of the seven gates to the underworld, Inanna must lose one piece of her raiment of power until she is naked and bowed low.

In this staged manner, Inanna abandons divinity, queenship, chastity, and religious authority until she is completely divested of her power, and therefore most at risk and her own identity most in question. This lack of protection allows Eriskigal to kill Inanna and turn her into a corpse, *a piece of meat*, which Eriskigal then hangs from a hook on the wall (Wolkstein & Kramer 1993, 60).

I weirdly love this part of the Inanna myth. However, it represents Inanna not only losing her life, but also her personhood. Demeter simply chose to turn herself into a crone; by comparison, Inanna's journey into disguise and loss of identity is pretty extreme.

NINSHUBUR'S SEARCH

Meanwhile, Ninshubur dresses as a beggar and goes to the father gods of the Sumerian pantheon one by one, requesting aid to resurrect Inanna. One by one, the gods deny Ninshubur, claiming that:

> "She who goes to the Dark City stays there."
>
> — WOLKSTEIN & KRAMER (1993)

Such a good line. Always gives me chills.

Eventually, Ninshubur approaches Father Enki, god of wisdom and Inanna's *mother's* father. Being wise, he knows of Inanna's importance to the survival of mankind (and that all the gods need human worship, which Inanna helps provide as she is goddess of earth as well as heaven).

So Enki agrees to help. He sends his minions to moan in sympathy with Eriskigal and garner her friendship and respect with empathy, so that they might request a boon of the death goddess. Charmed, Eriskigal offers them anything they desire. They request the corpse of Inanna and subsequently bring her back to life.

Another marker of the heroine: her strength is in networking – the family she has and the friends she makes.

Inanna is released from her entrapment in the underworld as a result of the empathic act of these minions sent to sympathize with Eriskigal. It is a sharing of feelings, empathy, that results in her release and continuation of her journey. This is a classic Heroine's Journey example of an act of sharing, of connection, resulting in positive continuation of the story.

Unfortunately for Inanna, the judges of the underworld insist that no one can return from death unscathed. So while they allow Eriskigal to fulfill her vow and send Inanna back, they insist that she do so with the *galla* (demons of the underworld) dogging her every move.

Patient and loving Ninshubur, waiting for her goddess to return, sees that Inanna is cursed with demons and throws herself at Inanna's feet, begging to be allowed to take on the demons for her. The *galla* happily agree to take Ninshubur in Inanna's place, but Inanna refuses on the grounds that Ninshubur is her constant support, her emotional succor, and her wise advisor. Ninshubur was willing to fight at her side and did not forget her, or her words. (Wolkstein & Kramer 1993, 69)

Inanna's two sons, both dressed as beggars, repeat this process, asking to take on Inanna's demons for her. Each time Inanna cries out her connection and love for them and will not let them sacrifice themselves.

Then she arrives back at the seat of her power, where she finds her husband, Dumuzi (god of shepherds), dressed in fine raiment and sitting on her throne in her place.

Enraged, Inanna throws him to the demons for his disloyalty and lack of love and his unwillingness to sacrifice for her. Essentially Inanna is punishing Dumuzi for separating himself from her. For a heroine there is no greater betrayal than an act of isolation in pursuit of superiority. The *galla* seize him and take him away.

INANNA'S SEARCH

There's a bit missing from the archaeological record here, but Dumuzi somehow escapes, and (chased by the *galla)* disappears somewhere in the realm of man. His sister Geshtinanna (goddess of wine, mind you) mourns him as lost.

The text picks up with the demons hunting Dumuzi and offering bribes to anyone who might reveal his whereabouts. Geshtinanna stays true and keeps his location secret, but one of his male friends betrays him.

Dumuzi is taken by the *galla* and as a result there's no butter or milk and "the shepfold was given to the winds" (Wolkstein & Kramer 1993, 84). Geshtinanna mourns her brother and Inanna is moved by her sister-in-law's sorrow and love. Inanna promises to rescue Dumuzi, but she does not know where he was taken.

A fly appears and offers to make a trade, as the fly knows Dumuzi's whereabouts. Inanna offers to allow the fly to hang out in beer houses learning all the wisdom and gossip, and, delighted by this boon, the fly tells all.

Inanna and Geshtinanna, together, find the weeping Dumuzi at the edges of the steppe.

INANNA'S ASCENT

Inanna brokers a deal with Eriskigal (and presumably the *galla*) whereby Geshtinanna (committed to her path of sisterly love and devotion) will spend half her time in the underworld in her brother's stead.

This yields up the classic end to a Heroine's Journey – compromise for the good of all. In this case, the sacred right of rebirth every New Year (see Kramer's notes on culture in Wolkstein & Kramer 1993, 125) is established representing the cycle of the seasons, consummation of marriage, and the continuation of civilization.

Inanna has both a visit to the underworld, sacrificing power and identity (she ends up a piece of meat on the wall, for goodness sake), *and* a search for reunification. As with all heroines, she is constantly assisted on her journey by family, sisterly devotion, and (in her particular case) a nosy fly with useful information.

Her ending is one of family and compromise, her strength is found in those times when she has assistance and aid, and her victory is neither violent nor predicated on the defeat of an enemy, but rather one of solidarity, hope, and rebirth.

This completes my retellings and breakdowns of three core myths underlying the Heroine's Journey.

In the next part, we'll discuss some of the *messages* and *themes* implied by these myths and look at two wildly successful pop culture examples of the Heroine's Journey in modern times: the Harry Potter novels and movies, and *The Twilight Saga*.

CHAPTER 5: HEROINE'S JOURNEY BEATS, THEMES & MESSAGES

Heroine's Journey basic beats

In this part, we will look at the previous myths as foundational examples of the Heroine's Journey, and how they are understood and reinterpreted in modern times in the context of storytelling. In other words, I'm a writer, so I want to understand the plot points and beats as a means toward manipulating reader desires.

> How can we take these core myths and activate them for a modern audience?

Your audience's expectations are rooted in the enduring nature of both heroic journeys, which form narrative psychological patterns as part of oral and then written traditions (not to mention art, music, theater, movies, television, and beyond) in the western world.

To some extent, these myths have become what readers expect from stories. Not all stories rely on one of these two journeys, but many of the most popular and best-selling stories in commercial genre fiction will and do.

———

Now that we've a mutual foundation of mythology to draw upon, here's the recap of the beats that make up a Heroine's Journey.

This time, I laid it out in three parts, each of which I've subdivided into a further four segments. This is not an outline, simply a general comprehension guide.

HEROINE'S JOURNEY BEATS

The Descent

Precipitated by a broken familial network.

Heroine's pleas ignored and she abdicates power.

Her withdrawal is *involuntary*.

Family offers aid but no solution.

The Search

The heroine's loss of family yields isolation/risk.

She employs disguise/subversion and alters her identity.

She appeals to and forms a surrogate network (found family).

She visits the underworld, aided by friends/family.

The Ascent

Success in her search results in a new or reborn familial network.

This ties to negotiation and compromise that will benefit all.

So that's the basic layout of a Heroine's Journey. Although, as with the Hero's Journey, no narrative necessarily contains them all, and no narrative must have them all (or in this order) to qualify as a Heroine's Journey.

It is possible to tap into expectations and resonate with readers merely by alluding to this structure, so long as you stick to the core notions of how your main character perceives and interacts with the other characters around her.

As storytellers, it behooves us to recognize that both journeys are flexible, the Heroine's perhaps even more than the Hero's because it has a more amorphous foundation (AKA fewer canonical myths and less reinforcement throughout time and within modern culture). It can be what we make of it.

Remember, for the heroine, revenge, retribution, and glory are unimportant. In fact, she tends to excel at portioning out tasks, achievements, and rewards. This is because of the way she perceives strength, power, and human interaction.

So with that in mind, let's move on to how some of the most popular versions of this journey invoked it.

NOTATION OF ABSENCE

In case you were terribly confused by the void

A brief detour before I begin the breakdown of themes and pop culture examples. I'd like to mention two of the Heroine's Journey models I'm *not* using in this book.

HEROINE'S JOURNEY: WOMAN'S QUEST FOR WHOLENESS

This is Maureen Murdock's Jungian-influenced psychological analysis of the Heroine's Journey (1990). The book mainly tackles a reinterpretation and pivoted feminist approach to the Hero's Journey (as presented by Joseph Campbell) and its patterns of withdrawal and return.

Murdock has a spiritual holistic stance with a psychoanalytic bent. If what you are looking for is an analysis of story in terms of beats, archetypes, tropes, themes, or messaging, then you may find this academic work a tad frustrating. It's probably worth going into if you're a literary writer or memoirist, or if you are on your own journey of self-discovery and you want a path toward understanding that particular application of mythological analysis.

45 MASTER CHARACTERS: MYTHIC MODELS FOR CREATING ORIGINAL CHARACTERS

Victoria Schmidt's version of the Heroine's Journey (2001) is based primarily on fairy tales, and is worth looking into if that's your particular interest or focus as a fiction author. Many writers find her book on the *45 Master Characters* useful. Outside of fairy tale retellings in fantasy and romance in particular, she's also used in screenwriting.

Her analysis seems based primarily on a model of inter-preting a solo journey of self-discovery, leaning more toward coming-of-age narratives. As such, her book might also be useful for those writing YA literature.

However, I'm not employing either approach here. Instead, I'm interested in using broader brush strokes to take a good hard look at the themes and narrative beats intrinsic to the Heroine's Journey (as seen in the three myths of **Chapter 4**) for storytellers and how modern pop culture has tackled them.

I prefer to focus on narration and story structure, and less on the internal struggles that make up the human emotional psyche. Of course, understanding such things can be very useful to writers, but this is the point where I say that focus is up to you to explore without me along for the ride. In other words, researching these other two possible foundations on your own is valuable, but not part of this book. Since these authors have provided other aspects, I've decided to take us on a different journey.

2

THINGS TO NOTICE

Tracking patterns of the heroine's narrative

As with a Hero's Journey analysis, and because themes can so easily become messages, I'm hoping that as I discuss the pop culture versions of this narrative that you can train yourself to notice certain prevailing themes populating (and defining) the Heroine's Journey through them.

INVOLUNTARY ACTION

The first theme to notice is that the descent at the beginning of a Heroine's Journey is an act imposed upon our heroine *involuntarily*. This precipitating launch device is usually a broken familial network when a lover, friend, or family member is taken or killed. The heroine's descent, as a result, moves her away from civilization and safety (and her seat of power) toward solitary, unacceptable risk. Remember, her strength is in her friends.

The more isolated she becomes, the weaker she is.

When a heroine's family is in danger, she will do anything to get them back, including abdicating her own position of power and authority.

However, even displaced from her role (be it goddess, queen, sorceress, fated savior, or wizard) she remains a civilizing force as she moves within her journey.

For example, even in Demeter's withdrawal as crone (punishing mankind with famine), she teaches a young man the secret of agriculture and gets a temple built. Isis trots about building multiple temples to Osiris even as she gathers the pieces of him together and learns how to mummify.

Unlike the hero, the heroine rarely descends into violence or extreme action when things don't go her way, or when faced with insurmountable odds.

In fact, if she is a tragic figure, she is more likely to go mad with disconnect and isolation.

POLITICAL POWER

When in possession of political power, the heroine acts more like a military general (or a really good general manager), getting help, recognizing the strengths in others, and doling out tasks and requests for aid accordingly. Her objective is often to build and empower in the form of community, city, family, love.

- Demeter: You go build me a temple. You go teach the children harvesting.
- Isis: You go invent mummification. You go kill your nasty uncle.

- Inanna: You go make me a throne. You go take on my demons.

RAPE IS A MISTAKE

A serious mistake many storytellers make with the Heroine's Journey is in choosing the rape of the heroine *herself* as the inciting event. Because this is not the severing of a familial network (it's happening to Demeter and not Persephone, so to speak), the resulting narrative can feel disingenuous, even polluted and clumsy.

The heroine *acts to save others*.

Her own rape as a motivation for action not only breaks a core narrative contract with readers, but it shows a gross misunderstanding of what rape actually does to the human psyche and what it means to the victim. In other words, stop using rape as a plot device to motivate your heroine. It's tired, overdone, and it doesn't work.

BREAKING THE CORE NETWORK

A key moment in any Heroine's Journey is that precipitating fracture of family that will drive her into action. For Demeter it is the loss of her daughter, for Isis the loss of her husband, and for Inanna the (eventual) loss of her husband.

In the upcoming examples, for Harry Potter it is delayed, but it's the loss of his family, first in death, and then in abandonment. For Bella of *Twilight* it's the loss of her mother, and then the prospective loss of her daughter, husband, and new vampire family.

WITHDRAWAL

While our hero tends to move toward objects and acquisitions of power (a supernatural sword, magic amulet, and so on), the heroine's descent is precipitated by a rejection of divine power (or defined social role) as a result of a familial connection (or relationship network) being taken from her. This can also be seen as a loss of identity or it can manifest in a more concrete way, such as an actual disguise.

- Demeter abdicates her power by throwing off her crown and descending from Mount Olympus.
- Isis also leaves her throne (and Isis also *is* the throne, so this is an abandonment of identity).
- Inanna leaves her tree-throne and sheds pieces of her raiment at each gate to the underworld.
- Harry Potter leaves the human world for Hogwarts. He also gets an invisibility cloak (like Demeter, he has more than one loss of identity).
- *Twilight*'s Bella emotionally withdraws, but also her entire search in the saga is one of identity through connection to others. She wishes to leave off being a human and become a vampire – she is trying to rebuild herself into the identity of a monster, and become unified with her man and his vampire family.

All these examples highlight a common marker of the Heroine's Journey: an element of disguise and of shifting identity in pursuit of reunification. Harry, in particular, does everything he does to learn more about his family, to help his new friends, and to save the world of wizards in which he finds himself (and the wonder that world engenders in him).

AID & NEW NETWORKS

As part of this search, our heroine finds second family, and pursues a constant need to further a relationship network (or the network finds her).

- Demeter receives aid from her sister, eventually is discovered by the daughters of a queen, and is adopted into their household as a nanny.
- Isis receives aid from her sister and nephew; she even networks herself into a family with the aid of her own... inventiveness, shall we call it?
- Inanna has her servant beg aid from Inanna's maternal grandfather.
- Harry has many surrogate family members, from siblings (Ron and Hermione) to avuncular characters like Hagrid, to various teachers and old family friends, not to mention the Weasleys.
- Bella's own father keeps trying to help her, as do her new school friends, and a whole werewolf pack tries to aid her before she finds her way firmly into the bosom of vampire kind. (Or do I say *fangs of vampire kind*?)

Like female characters in the Hero's Journey, male characters in the Heroine's Journey (such as Hades, Helios, Hermes, or Zeus) are often underdeveloped archetypes of masculinity (the villain, traitorous friend/family member, trickster guide, and father figure respectively) and tend to be one-dimensional in the context of the narrative as a result. This is something that we writers should be aware of and attempt to mitigate. It contributes to readers responding negatively to villainous characters in particular, and describing them in reviews as one-dimensional.

CIVILIZING FORCE

Even as the heroine searches, displaced from her role (be it goddess, queen, sorceress, fated savior, special one, or wizard) she remains a civilizing force as she moves within her journey.

- Demeter and Isis build.
- Inanna consolidates power and reclaims her throne.
- Harry doles out the wisdom he has learned and delegates roles to his new friends. He helps his team or house win, yet always tries to share the glory.
- Bella is perhaps less cognizant of her role as a civilizing force, but she does bring the vampires together. She acts to unify them against evil and oppression. She even gets the werewolves to fight alongside.

Like with Demeter and Isis, there is certainly a theme in *The Twilight Saga* of the appeal of structures (the honeymoon house, the marriage cottage, the vampires' house in the woods, and so forth) that lends itself to the notion of building things together, safety in numbers and establishing a home.

COMPROMISE

The final important narrative element in a Heroine's Journey is positive compromise.

Our heroine is good at it, and that is a good thing, because her ability to negotiate will result in an integration of power, and a positive impact on the world and civilization. Demeter and Inanna negotiate for the balance of the seasons, and Isis for life and afterlife. With our two modern examples, as with the mythological ones, compromise happens at the very end. Bella and her vampires form a nonviolent parlay with the bad vampires (Volturi) and the local werewolf pack that allows them to keep their child and family. Harry casts aside the ultimate power of the elder wand so that he may have a normal life with his friends and create a family for himself.

This compromise always occurs in the final chapter of the journey; for a series, that means the end of the final book.

In terms of broader patterns, as with the Hero's Journey's cycles of withdrawal and return, the Heroine's Journey can have patterns of networking, attempts at reunification, and establishment of found family that are repeated again and again. These may be physical, mental, or emotional.

The heroine seeks to unite with what was lost.

Her definition of a *successful* journey, therefore, is in *connection*.

A heroine will compromise to achieve that goal. This is not a weakness. This is the very definition of what makes her a strong protagonist within the framework of this journey.

> Her definition of *power*, therefore, is nested in information gathering and community.

When you write your heroine in crisis, yes, you can absolutely subdue her enemy, but then she is more likely to turn them to her side, persuade them to give up, or trap them away than she is to kill them.

Revenge, glory, the death of an enemy, recognition of accomplishments, or presentation of a boon (while these may occur) are *irrelevant* to the heroine's core identity. What motivates and matters to our heroine is being reunited with what was lost, usually in a covenant form that benefits all.

If you're reading this because you've read one of my books or series, you'll have seen that I do this all the time. Alexia in *Soulless* begins her journey in isolation, purposeless, and is therefore useless and ineffective. It is through her friends and connections and the love of a grumpy werewolf (and eventually his whole pack) that she succeeds on her journey and finds her place in the world surrounded by family.

Because my main characters find power and solace through their friends, readers are particularly attracted to those side characters. They love them because she does. She loves them, as a heroine, because they are her strength. Developing a supportive friendship group in your stories is a powerful way to resonate with readers who seek comfort in their entertainment.

There are other themes to unpack as well, but I'm starting with these ones, as they are particularly key markers of a Heroine's Journey.

3

HEROINE'S JOURNEY EXAMPLE 1

Harry Potter and the Philosopher's Stone

Am I saying J. K. Rowling wrote the Harry Potter books with the Heroine's Journey in mind? No.

But you can certainly see it, if you know what to look for. And it's an excellent counterexample to something like *Wonder Woman*, in that it showcases a male heroine. So that's why I chose it.

Also, I want you to see how very commercially viable this journey can be – how it can transform a generation.

For this first example, I'll be using the first book (or movie, if you prefer) in the Harry Potter franchise (*Harry Potter and the Philosopher's Stone*, 1997). But each book in the series (as well as the series as a whole) holds together under the umbrella of the Heroine's Journey. Occasionally, therefore, I'll also be referring to events at the very end of this series and speaking of all the books as a completed, single story arc, since the ultimate ending is often key to understanding which journey a piece of pop culture is utilizing.

I chose Harry Potter because the franchise is culturally significant, commercially successful, and an almost too ideal example of a Heroine's Journey. It also represents several genres that make use of the Heroine's Journey a lot – fantasy (specifically portal fantasy and urban fantasy) and YA literature in a school setting.

HARRY'S DESCENT

We start off with basically all of Harry's family being killed. His pleas (such as they are – he's a squalling baby) are ignored and he involuntarily abdicates all power. Literally, he rendered powerless: his knowledge of the wizarding world is disallowed as he's placed among humans (muggles). He doesn't even know what he is. So another trope of the Heroine's Journey is spotlighted here: loss of identity.

His descent is, clearly, involuntary. His extended Dursley family in the form of aunt, uncle, and cousin offer him aid (such as it is), but this is not the solution to his need to find, understand, and reunite with his lost family, and by extension, the wizarding world.

The end result for Harry is isolation (for a heroine, that means danger and risk), and we get that enduring image of loneliness – Harry locked in his cupboard under the staircase. Harry's positive way forward from then on (not to mention his path of strength, identity, and understanding) will always be toward connection, friendship, and family.

HARRY'S SEARCH

Harry must now undertake his search for unity, finding what was lost and taken from him – his family, his magical powers, and his past. However, to do so he must leave the Dursleys, and abdicate the mortal world by being compelled to go to Hogwarts. We then have a series of Harry's appeals to surrogate family and networks for connection – from his friendship with Hagrid to Ron and Hermione, to adoption into his Hogwarts House, to joining a sports team.

He makes a few ill-advised appeals as well, such as when he first sees his heart's greatest desire (his lost nuclear family) in the Mirror of Erised. It is interesting to note that Harry finds this mirror on his own – a danger – as opposed to being given the photo album by a member of his network later – an assist. This is, of course, our heroine attempting to rebuild his lost community.

In this first book, Harry is given the ultimate in disguise, subversion, and identity-changing capacity: the invisibility cloak, which he immediately makes use of. After all, he's a heroine.

In *Harry Potter and the Philosopher's Stone*, Harry then engages in a visit to the underworld. By this I mean the trap door he must get through is guarded by a massive three-headed dog, Fluffy. (Or should I call him Cerberus? We've moved past allegory to direct mythological reference.) On his journey into the underworld, Harry is aided by friends: Hermione beats a plant and logic-puzzle and Ron beats a chess game. This in turn allows Harry to retrieve the stone.

Harry not only listens to the advice of his friends – Hermione's advice includes the importance of friendship – but also proves his worth in the arenas that he can control, like flying to catch the door key.

There isn't an ending battle sequence to this first book. It's more a kind of emotionally based passive resistance as Harry retrieves the stone using the mirror that's meant to *show him his heart's desire*. Then he tries to run.

And guess who comes to bolster him through his confrontation with Voldemort?

His dead parents, of course, erroneously offered as a lure by Voldemort, who sees power only in superiority. Harry then defeats his enemy through touch – intimacy.

Once more with feeling – what do we have? Strength through connection!

All of these are defining characteristics of the Heroine's Journey in beats and plot, not to mention sentiment and emotional resonance. The Harry Potter books, more than anything else, are about the sensation of *belonging*. Which is one of the many reasons why they have such broad appeal.

HARRY'S ASCENT

Next we would expect an ascent for Harry (as the heroine) and he should engage in a negotiation for reunification and compromise. This occurs in the hospital with Dumbledore after Harry wakes up from his underworld ordeal. Turns out the stone, which would have been the all-important boon in a Hero's Journey, is destroyed without fuss. After all, our heroine is not interested in glory or physical representations of victory.

This is echoed throughout the final books with the destruction of the horcruxes. In return, Harry is given the connection he craves – the affection of his fellow students, the knowledge of his friends' wellbeing, the story of his parents' death, and the reason for his scar and his situation.

The ultimate compromise, and key to this being a Heroine's Journey, is the fact that Harry now knows that his mother's sacrifice was for love, the ultimate connection and strength. This will set Harry on his path as heroine going forward, always looking to find family and prove himself worthy of that love.

Dumbledore sets himself up as both surrogate father and mentor. This goes beyond simply foreshadowing that he's most likely to die during the course of this series (because no one just leaves the mentor archetype alone). Also, he is providing Harry with a new network, one at Hogwarts. His friends and teachers are his new family. As Harry says at the end of the movie when he leaves for the Dursley house, he's not going home (the implication being that Hogwarts is now his true home).

So, the themes present that reinforce this book and series as a Heroine's Journey are threefold:

First, for Harry, revenge is irrelevant. It's never about killing Voldemort. Harry isn't jonesing to take down Voldemort using extreme violence as recompense for Harry's parents' deaths. If he were on a Hero's Journey, Harry would be motivated primarily by a need for retribution and victory, and he would want that responsibility and glory for himself alone.

Second, Harry shares his glory. At the end of the first book, he shares (involuntarily, but still) winning the house cup not only with Ron and Hermione, but also with Neville Longbottom. This is a pattern that repeats throughout the series.

At the very end of the entire story arc, it is Ron, Hermione, and Neville who take out the final horcruxes. Harry would never have succeeded on his journey without his friends. Harry also then throws away the most powerful wand in the world (or in the books, returns it to Dumbledore's grave). Talk about a main character not interested in symbols or actualities of ultimate power. (I mean, come on, it's the sword of the father figure being rejected. Can you imagine what King Arthur would have to say about *that*?)

Similarly, Harry is always most in danger when he is abandoned by his friends, when he is alone, and even then, the ghosts of his dead family usually come to his aid (yeah, more family!). This is not because he is weak, it is because Harry is a heroine, and his success is nested in the networks he forms and the friendships he makes – these remain solid and strong even in death. This emphasis on family support is also one of the major reasons these books are so beloved. It is a constantly repeated refrain often voiced by characters – that Harry has friends and he is not alone.

Which brings us to the third way we know these books and movies are Heroine's Journeys – scenes of power. Diametrically opposed to a movie like *Wonder Woman*, Harry Potter shows pivotal moments of power or solidarity in group scenes and shots. He is always with friends or school chums.

Throughout the franchise, depictions of strength and courage are wrapped in togetherness, from winning the house cup, to final battle sequences, to quidditch matches. Harry's sense of cooperation and fair play is so ingrained that even in the midst of a competition like the Triwizard Tournament, he does none of the tasks without help, and ends with suggesting that he and Cedric Diggory take the cup (boon) together.

Everything always ends with Harry reconnected – to new family, to found family, and in solidarity with other characters who have remained strong and supportive all along. The final scene of the final movie is of Harry, Ron, Hermione, and their families in a negotiated reunification of the wizard world – for the good of all.

He saved the wizarding world... but he did it with help, and for the benefit of everyone.

4

HEROINE'S JOURNEY EXAMPLE 2

Twilight

Next, I'll be covering *The Twilight Saga* (books and movies) as our second example of the Heroine's Journey drawn from popular culture. I'll be tackling this one in the context of both the first book and as the whole series.

Unlike the Harry Potter series, for *The Twilight Saga*, the Heroine's Journey is only self-contained in the first book, *Twilight*, and to some extent the final book, *Breaking Dawn*. The series as a whole is a Heroine's Journey, but not the middle books individually. The middle two books, *New Moon* and *Eclipse*, are mostly a heroine's Search in the context of the overarching narrative, without the bracketing of Descent (which, looking at the whole saga, mainly occurs in the first book) and Ascent (which, looking at the whole saga, mainly occurs in the final book).

Again, *Twilight* and the final book, *Breaking Dawn,* are basically self-contained three-part Heroine's Journeys, but the middle two books are not.

Incidentally, writers, breaking up the journey like this is one way to draw out tension across a series. It means the middle books act like cliffhangers for the overarching Heroine's Journey. It is one of the reasons that readers find this series so addictive.

———

No matter how you feel personally about *The Twilight Saga*, it was profoundly culturally impactful and commercially successful. I've chosen it for that reason, and also because it's primarily a fantasy meets coming-of-age teen romance, and these genres (fantasy, romance, and YA) utilize the Heroine's Journey a great deal.

BELLA'S DESCENT

Twilight opens with Bella leaving Phoenix, a big city in the desert, for a small town in the Pacific Northwest. There is a kind of color and temperature to her descent as she leaves the super saturated, bright warmth of Phoenix (and her mother's flighty fondness) for the dark, rainy gloom of the coastal forests (and her awkward, estranged father).

Her descent continues into a new school full of unknowns in which she receives unwanted attention and encounters Edward, whom she finds both attractive and scary (hel-loooo Byronic archetype, see **Chapter 7**). We also learn that there is an existential threat in the form of murders nearby.

Throughout the series, Bella constantly copes with familial networks and lovers being taken or broken via a descent of some kind (her estranged relationship with her own parents and their divorce is an interesting twist on this). Usually her descents are emotional or mental or both, deep dives into depression and introversion. Her pleas are ignored (again, these are often depressive and introspective sentimental pleas).

She engages in multiple abdications of power (sometimes through the simple act of passive resistance). She does this by sinking into depression, taking to her room or her bed, walking alone in the forest or in cities, diving off cliffs into the sea, or taking a wild motorcycle ride with a thug. In other words, acting out as any teenager denied her desire might well do.

Her descents are usually involuntary (depression, hopelessness, sadness). Her family offers aid (trying to talk to her, call her, take her out for a meal) but to no avail, and generally this results in a dangerous isolation. Since Bella's main motivation is a hunt for a new familial network (literally in the guise of a vampire family, husband, and child), isolation is particularly risky for her.

Considering the series as a whole, the first book/movie, *Twilight,* is also the Descent for the larger saga, as it shows Bella moving into the world of vampires and the supernatural. It also depicts her falling in love with Edward and the possibility of eternal love that he represents.

During this first book, she learns that what she truly desires is to become a vampire herself. This will precipitate her major Search that characterizes the middle books of the series.

BELLA'S SEARCH

Bella's initial search in *Twilight* begins after Edward saves her from being hit by a car with his super strength. This search is one of discovery – what is Edward? She begins dreaming of him as well as confronting him about his behavior. Clues are dropped in the narrative, like the fact that Edward and his family do not go to school on sunny days. When Bella is off shopping, she goes looking for a book about vampires on her own (isolation, risk) and is nearly attacked/raped. Edward rescues her.

Funny note: I'm always amused to find that in this book we see Bella searching in the literal Internet sense as well. Heh heh.

Eventually, Bella voices to Edward what he is (showing that her information has been successfully gathered and prospective future needs understood), and they show up at school together as a unit – solidarity. Classic Heroine's Journey manifestations of connection and networking.

Bella then confesses her love and begins her second search, the one that will drive the rest of the series, that of becoming a vampire herself so she may be with Edward forever. It's also revealed that vampires have powers. Edward can read minds, but he cannot read Bella's – she is special.

Incidentally, a lot of these notions of specialness and fate are Gothic tropes and archetypes, and yeah, they'll come up again later.

Bella engages in multiple quests for unity, her end goal to be with Edward (connected) and become a vampire and part of his family unit (networked). Every time she loses connection to that community and goal (be it vampires, werewolves, or school chums), she is at risk.

- In *Twilight,* this happens when the bad vampire

threatens Bella's mother and she goes alone to confront him. She is nearly killed and Edward barely manages to save her.

- In *New Moon*, after Edward rejects her and the vampires leave, Bella descends into an emotional depression and self-isolation that once again puts her at risk (near suicide and self-destructive tendencies).

Throughout the series, Bella also engages in various appeals to family and attempts to rebuild community. In *New Moon*, this is offered up in the guise of Jacob and the local werewolf pack. After Jacob also rejects her by severing their nascent relationship, Bella jumps off a cliff, descending underwater – an excellent allegory for the underworld, as this is a physical attempt at death.

Considering the saga as a whole, the middle two books/movies and the first part of the final installment make up the majority of Bella's main Search – eternal life as a means to becoming one with Edward and the family his vampire coven represents. Wrapped up in this is her near constant acquisition of more family (surrogate and otherwise) in the form of the werewolves, marriage, and eventually her own child.

BELLA'S ASCENT

In *Twilight*, Bella's ascent occurs after the battle with the evil vampire, where Bella is bitten and nearly turned/killed. As with the first Harry Potter book, our main character awakens in a hospital. In Bella's case, her biological mother and father are there to symbolize reconnection. She reconciles with her father, goes to prom, and recognizes that what she really wants is to be a vampire with Edward forever (her next Search). We end *Twilight* with both a kiss and an implied looming threat.

Considering the saga as a whole, Bella's major ascent occurs after her child is born and her Search is complete; in other words, after she herself becomes a vampire. In this way the climax of *Breaking Dawn* is both a formation of the unbreakable family unit (symbolized by the child) and the establishment of an eternal connection to divinity and love (in the form of Edward and his vampire family).

This is why the birth and resurrection sequence (yes, *resurrection*) is so powerful and resonates so profoundly with readers. As do the scenes directly afterward, where Bella awakens empowered and reunifies with her daughter, her husband, her vampire family, and the scope of her newfound vampire abilities.

And what are those abilities?

Shielding and the power to control her own vampire hunger! Defense, not offense.

Why?

Because she is a heroine.

What does a heroine want to do more than anything else?

Protect.

The remainder of the final book is the Ascent to compromise, or Bella figuring out a way to preserve her new unit by reaching out to even more vampires, by trying to understand what her child really is, and by determining a way to reconcile with the Volturi (who would destroy her, her child, and her family).

Because this is a Heroine's Journey, we know that this compromise will reshape the world, or at least the vampires' world, in a manner that allows the integration and safety of Bella's network, which by the end of the series includes her vampire in-laws, her human family, her werewolf surrogate family, her daughter, and her husband.

The final battle sequence in the series against the Volturi is particularly indicative of a Heroine's Journey. The Volturi, in their mad need to collect all the best powers into one group, are themselves a bastardization of a hero-ine's need for familial networking. This makes for an effective enemy for a heroine, as they foil Bella's own desires in a corrupted form. In the climactic battle scene, for one thing, there turns out to be no real violence at all.

This franchise is often criticized for this dream sequence approach, when in fact it's a device used to demonstrate a fate worse than death for our heroine. What's that fate, for both Bella and the Volturi? Having all familial networks taken away or destroyed in an effort to physi-cally defeat an enemy.

For any heroine (good or evil), nothing is worse than a Pyrrhic victory (i.e., a victory, but with so many losses that winning hardly matters, as there is nothing left to fight for).

In the case of this series, Bella's negotiation for reunifica-tion is delegated to Alice (as the mad prophetess, see upcoming discussion of archetypes), and the resulting compromise benefits the world. But Bella's reason for undertaking this aspect of her journey is to protect her family – her child, her vampire husband, and the continued existence of her kind of vampires (the abstainers).

The saga ends with Bella's family network firmly established and her place amongst the vampires assured. Revenge against the Volturi is irrelevant (in fact, it's explicitly verboten), and glory is irrelevant (as the glorious battle never even occurs in reality). This is reassuring both to the characters and to the readers.

As we might expect from a Heroine's Journey, depictions of power, joy, and the final sequences all occur as familial groups or as couples. The very ending of *The Twilight Saga* movies is particularly indicative of a romance story, where the codified power of unity is represented by a couple in a romantic encounter (in the romance genre, this is usually marriage or sex, or both).

For storytellers, the tactic is clear; the heroine is in a position of greatest strength when she is in a group, therefore the most powerful scenes in a novel of this kind (particularly romance) will be those depicting moments of mental (often dialogue driven), emotional, or physical intimacy with another person (or persons).

This is why engagements, weddings, parties, and sex scenes are so important in Heroine's Journey narratives – they tend to highlight all three kinds of intimacy at once.

ADDITIONAL EXAMPLES OF THE HEROINE

Just a few more so you have a range of comparison

In addition to the two I've already described in depth, here are a few more examples of the Heroine's Journey that I've noticed over the years: space operas like *Star Trek: The Next Generation* (1987); most sitcoms; all romantic comedies AKA romcoms, and YA romances, like *Love, Simon* (2018) or *To All the Boys I've Loved Before* (2014); so-called female empowerment comedies, like *Girls Trip* (2017); lighter hearted caper movies and heist shows, like *Leverage* (2008); and most media concerning superhero *teams*, like *Supergirl* the TV show (2015).

On the page, the Heroine's Journey can be found in all romance novels; most cozy mysteries (I have brought you all together, here, today, because one of you is a *murderer*); some SF/F, particularly those with a group dynamic back-bone, like space opera; a great deal of so-called women's fiction, like *Waiting to Exhale*; and at least half of all YA.

Why is it important for you to understand examples like these when creating your stories?

Because they are commercially successful and do it well. If you read or watch only a few of these with the foundation of the Heroine's Journey in mind, you can see how the journey has been manipulated for a modern audience and develop tricks of your own, toward a cleaner, sharper plot. Also, if you're suffering from any kind of writer's block, a few of these may give you ideas on how to get out of the hole you have written yourself into.

I'm not advising you to be derivative; I am saying you might be inspired.

HEROINE'S JOURNEY HIDDEN MESSAGES

Really fascinating nitty-gritty

There are enduring narrative elements and messages in the Heroine's Journey that I think are important for writers to recognize.

HOW THE HEROINE'S JOURNEY VIEWS MOTIVATION

The first thing for a storyteller to think about when writing a heroine is that her descent away from power or safety is rarely voluntary at the start. She takes action to help others. A heroine undertakes her journey as a result of a familial network being severed. Her need to mend that breach is what drives her into motion.

If you want to set your heroine into motion quickly, take someone she values away from her – lover, sister, friend, companion, child, mother, niece or nephew. Or, if it has to be an object that is taken, not a person, make certain that object has a profound familial connection – a diary, journal, photo album, family spell-book, mother's enchanted teacup, and so forth.

A quick word on this plot point. To many authors, the very idea of *action happening to the main character* is abhorrent. This is also roundly criticized by educators and critics (with the possible exception of situational comedy).

I need to stress that being driven into action by outside elements is not the same as being *passive* or *reactive*. Even if it were, I've considered making the case that critics, writing workshops, and creative writing teachers have been trained into a negative perception of reactive behavior in main characters by an excessive reliance on and prioritization of the Hero's Journey. After all, the perception of passivity as a *negative* is endemic to *that* mythos, not this one.

Either way, it is possible to write your heroine without everything happening *to* her.

> Her descent may be involuntary, but the actions that result in order to reconnect her with the world, how she goes into motion from that descent onward, those are her choices and her decisions.

Additionally, a heroine doesn't *refuse the call*, if indeed there is one.

Why?

Because her family has been taken from her! She's not going to be coy about pursuing a reunification. She isn't a hero and that's not her pattern.

Once a heroine goes into action, she stays that way unless isolated.

HOW THE HEROINE'S JOURNEY VIEWS FEMININITY

Feminine characters (and again, by that I mean characters *gendered* feminine by the narrative, not necessarily biologically female characters) appear as foils, siblings, friends, and lovers, and they will almost always *assist* the heroine through motivation, emotional support, and the tendering of useful information (espionage and gossip for the win).

This is one of the reasons I wrote my Finishing School series about female spies: This concept makes for a very happy marriage under the Heroine's Journey umbrella.

The feminine, therefore, represents a largely *positive* element in this journey, which stands in stark contrast to the Hero's Journey, where the feminine appearing as archetypes usually represent civilization, stasis, and obstacle – and, by its implication of stopping a hero from completing his quest, is *negative*.

HOW THE HEROINE'S JOURNEY VIEW ISOLATION

The next thing storytellers can make use of is the fact that, for the heroine, loneliness and solitary actions are dangerous.

There's a reason Harry fears the dementors over and above all other monsters. They epitomize a heroine's definition of loss and despair – aloneness. It's a near perfect execution of this journey that Harry's weapon against dementors, insofar as it is a *weapon,* is a symbol of both love and family (Harry's Patronus represents his father, both emotionally within the context of the story, and in the root of the word itself, *patron*).

HOW THE HEROINE'S JOURNEY VIEWS STRENGTH

Here is a tool by which more storytellers can use the Heroine's Journey to significant impact.

Because a heroine's strength is in her network, community and civilization are desirable, including concrete symbols thereof – from organized religion to nesting and building a home to organizing a party or celebration. As writers of this journey, it behooves us to give our audience multiple likable characters assisting our heroine, but also to describe her comforting physical spaces (Ron's family home, Bella and Edward's cabin), not to mention community building events (family dinners, friendship gatherings, weddings, childbirth, and group workplaces).

- Give your heroine multiple, likable friends who do not betray her.
- Give her the opportunity to help and provide for those friends, and for them to help her in turn.
- Give her the chance to shine in a group, at work, at a party, in a relationship, with her family.

This can be a small thing – perhaps she has a really beautiful home, or perhaps as the book progresses her home becomes more beautiful, calm, and welcoming.

Perhaps she teaches a self-defense class, or excels in a lifelong pursuit that requires a team, like general contractor or interior design, or running a bakery or being the CEO of a social games development company.

HOW THE HEROINE'S JOURNEY VIEWS COMMUNICATION

Another tool in your toolbox of the Heroine's Journey?

Dialogue!

Writing this journey means leaning into dialogue a lot. After all, the primary power tool for building intimacy between characters is to have them, you know, *talk* to each other.

If you are an author who finds dialogue easy to write, if you see those two characters like a film in your head talking to each other, then the Heroine's Journey is your friend. If dialogue is not your strength, you might consider researching techniques and paying close attention to well-executed movie scripts.

HOW THE HEROINE'S JOURNEY VIEWS SUCCESS

More tools: show compromise and define that as success.

Next thing to remember when writing a Heroine's Journey is that connection will be achieved through compromise, and that compromise will benefit all, not just the heroine – even if that *all* is defined only as her greater friendship group (as it will be in most contemporary romances), her small town or city community (cozy mysteries, urban fantasies) and not an upgrade to the entire world (YA, epic fantasy) or universe (science fiction).

Have your heroine compromise, and highlight this in a positive light.

The prevailing theme of how we define success is also key to writing this journey well. For our heroine, friendship and found family signify safety, and safety is better than glory. A heroine *succeeds* by building a network. For her, the very definition of success therefore is *unity*.

In other words, your main character's motivation can help you determine which journey you are writing. So, take a moment to sit down and ask yourself this question:

> What does my main character really want? Physically? Mentally? Emotionally?

Which brings us to the messaging of your narrative.

HOW THE HEROINE'S JOURNEY VIEWS DELEGATING

The prevailing positive message throughout a Heroine's Journey is that asking for (or needing) help is *good*.

I know that's a hard one for the western mindset to grapple with, but for a heroine, getting help is not a weakness. It is the very definition of her best strength. This may be something she is unaware of at the start of her journey, but it should be made clear to readers.

In the Harry Potter series, this is done through consistently ending books with Harry in a group dynamic with his friends, hugging Hagrid. Harry is depicted being celebrated amongst his peers in moments of pride and euphoria, but his best moments are quiet familial ones, with the Weasleys, on the train platform at the very end.

One way to show this in writing is to depict your heroine as a delegator, identifying complementary abilities and activating them in the context of creating a cohesive whole for a mutually beneficial outcome.

Harry's friends often self-delegate, taking on the tasks they feel best suit them, like Ron and the chess game, or Hermione and her research. Her weapons, if she has them, are usually defensive in nature, as her networking objective is best met with protection. Some of Harry's best spells and the ones particularly important for him to pass along to his friends? The Patronus and Expelliarmus spells – both of which are defensive (shielding and disarming respectively). I actually crowed in delight when Bella's vampire power was revealed to be a *shield*. (I mean, come on! How perfectly heroine is that? Argh, so on point.)

There is a reason I made my main character Alexia the supernatural equivalent of an electrical ground. Her power is not really to *do* anything to her enemies, but simply to cancel them out – an inward-focused ability, if you will. I went even more heroine with one of my other main characters, Prudence, who has the ability to take away and then take on supernatural abilities – in other words, a kind of sharing of power. How heroine is that?

HOW THE HEROINE'S JOURNEY VIEWS POWER

Finally, let's think about power when we write.

Our heroine's depictions of power will occur in groups or as part of a couple. Since the heroine's focus is on maintaining community, someone else usually goes off and slays her enemies or makes her requests for her (see Isis and Horus, Inanna and Ninshubur, or Demeter and Hermes). Her journey is never about death, revenge, or retribution. She rarely (if ever) ends up alone.

A quick note before you think I'm glorifying this journey and slamming the Hero's. Yes, I do believe the emphasis on solitary action, self-sacrifice, and never asking for help in the Hero's Journey is damaging to modern society (and I will talk about this more).

The myth of the rugged individual has been canonized as a particularly American trait for centuries, in a manner that makes *going it alone* and *doing it yourself* something glorious and desirable. This has led us to a place where asking for help, particularly if you are a male identified individual, is seen as weak or feminine. Simultaneously this correlates *weak* with *feminine*, and *strength* with *isolation*.

We are collectively dealing with the consequences of having created a space where males are vilified for wanting to care for others – for seeking connection through communication, touch, or emotional resonance.

But that doesn't let the Heroine's Journey off the hook (pun intended when thinking about Inanna). The above discussion concerning depictions of power can result in some seriously damaging messages being disseminated by the Heroine's Journey too, if mishandled by storytellers. Particularly when gender and biological sex are conflated.

For example, the prevailing message underpinning far too many older romance novels is that to be *complete* (powerful and successful) a *woman* must be coupled to a *man*. This removes the gendered nature of the narrative (remember, our heroine doesn't have to be female) and pushes it into the biological sexual sphere. We end up with such distressing concepts as a troubled alpha dude who only needs to sleep with the *correct* woman to turn righteous and loving. In slang terms, we call that a *pussy salvation* narrative in bad-boy romances. It pops up all the time (pun intended).

Similarly, because a heroine is in danger when isolated (which can be very tense and exciting in the context of the story, and yes, you should use this fact as you write to add tension), she can be shown wallowing overmuch in that isolation to the point of attempting suicide due to social rejection, over-romanticizing the idea of her requiring a man to rescue her.

Not very nice messages.

So do keep in mind that there are minefield messages to be had in either narrative when you are exploring manifestations of power in particular.

It is interesting to note, however, that the Heroine's Journey (particularly as exemplified by the romance genre) is far more vilified than the Hero's by critics and pundits for disseminating its messages. Just think about what it's like to say you write romance novels at a cocktail party and you'll understand what I mean.

What I'm hoping you're asking yourself at this juncture is *why* that might be the case. Romance novelists, and to a lesser extent fantasy and YA novelists, are up against a social stigma around the Heroine's Journey, whether they or their accusers realize this or not.

So let's delve into that a little, shall we? Because this next part will help you, as an author, handle the consequences of choosing to write this journey as a professional and as a brand.

CHAPTER 6: HEROINE'S JOURNEY GETS DEVALUED

Delving into data

In 2016, some data burst onto the writing world. The details have been contested since then, but it did lay out some interesting statistics that, if perhaps not exactly correct, put numbers in play that are still worth discussing.

I am, of course, referring to Data Guy's Author Earnings Report, particularly with reference to romance fiction, which was presented at the RWA National Conference in 2016 (using data gathering in 2015). The report itself is no longer available online, and Data Guy has since shut down the Author Earnings site. But you can search for information about it and the resulting discussion to your heart's content.

Essentially, Data Guy's 2016 report told us many things about the United States book industry, not the least of which was that roughly half of physical *print* book readers surveyed consumed fiction, and of that half, about 4.4 percent read romance in physical print book form. In the digital (ebook) arena, however, romance makes up at least *half* of *all* fiction read. Data Guy's analysis (which focused on Amazon.com in the USA) found that 45 percent of all digital books sold were romance.

Even if you don't believe Data Guy, Nielsen reported that 29 percent of fiction sales in 2015 could be attributed to romance – combined print and digital. (Information available online using this redirect: gailcarriger.com/HJ_romance)

Print and ebook circulation data from *Library Journal* (2019) found romance to be the fourth most popular fiction genre, after mystery, general fiction, and thrillers. (Information available online using this redirect: gailcarriger.com/HJ_library)

Any way you look at it, a huge number of readers in the United States (which is also the biggest English language market for books) read romance.

Did you know this? If you did know, did it really register that romance occupies this much market share?

Add in other examples of the Heroine's Journey (like many YA, most cozies, and a lot of comedy), and one might argue that the Heroine's Journey is just as popular, if not more so, than the Hero's Journey.

So now that we understand that the Heroine's Journey can be huge in terms of commercial success, popularity, readership, and bottom line, we find that romance in particular is grossly undervalued in the book industry and in popular discourse.

This is partly to do with the fact that romance is fast-moving and embraced digital editions and independent author publishing before most other genres. Data Guy's 2016 report states that 89 percent of romance sales are digital, and 67 percent aren't even tracked by traditional industry metrics.

Romance is also profoundly understudied by academics. It's roundly criticized, dismissed, and frowned upon by critics, awards committees, author residencies, and other gatekeepers of literary authority. It has been since its inception, when romance was born out of the Gothic literary movement.

Romance is also the primary bastion of the Heroine's Journey. Perhaps I am conflating two things that might not be intrinsically linked – although they are, in my estimation, so I shall stick to my guns.

WHY DO WE DISMISS THE HEROINE'S JOURNEY SO READILY?

Well, the Heroine's Journey emphasizes and supports narrative elements, themes, and messages that western cultures perceive as subjectively weak in the context of the Hero's Journey. Also, genres focusing on this journey are mostly written and consumed by women.

I'm sorry, but there isn't a kinder way of putting this:

The Heroine's Journey is dismissed and critically abused because of widescale codified and indoctrinated misogyny (for more evidence of this, read the cited article by Carpenter 2019).

As a career writer of this journey, this situation is going to put you in a defensive position, often socially. Like Harry with his Patronus and Bella with her shield powers, you'll need to gird yourself. I highly recommend that, like any heroine, you build yourself a powerful group of writer friends. Ones who also write these kinds of journeys and are happy to counsel you not only on points of plot and writing, but on the emotional repercussions of an embattled career path.

I said I wasn't going to get psychological, but it turns out I am.

A great deal of writing is lonely.

It's one of the reasons introverts gravitate to this profession. But if the heroine teaches us anything, it's that in loneliness lies danger. Whether it's you the storyteller, or your protagonist, please learn to ask for help when you need it. Learn to see that as a strength. There are wonderful online groups and peer mentoring options, local writers' groups and author organizations. Even dragging yourself to the occasional conference or convention can work wonders.

I've learned over the years to be proud of what I write. To say, when asked, that I write commercial genre fiction, mostly the Heroine's Journey, always with romantic elements. And that it sells. It brings readers comfort and makes them happy. And that is something to find strength in.

HEROINE'S JOURNEY OUT OF FOCUS

How we damage our own culture

The Heroine's Journey emphasizes the following:

- networking
- connection
- solidarity and unity
- asking for help
- giving aid
- success through portioning out achievement

All of these, under the umbrella of the Hero's Journey, will be regarded as weak, inefficient, and failures of solo achievement (even, occasionally, cheating).

The Heroine's Journey also generally contains comedy, which is easy to dismiss and trivialize. Comedy is rarely taken seriously, praised, or given critical acclaim – it is, after all, *comedic*. How many comedy films have won top-billed Academy Awards, for example, in the last twenty years? I would argue only *Shakespeare in Love* fully qualifies, and even it doesn't have a Heroine's Journey happy ending.

Because of its emphasis on connection, a Heroine's Journey (even if it is not a romance) often has a romantic thread, which is not to say this trope can't be damaging in its effect on readers' expectations of their own lives. Such concepts in romance as *the one* or *fated mates* conflict with more practical notions of compromise and relationships being hard work.

There's also an inclination to glorify marriage or sexual partnership over being single.

Finally, the Heroine's Journey usually ends happily, which critics like to see as twee or pat or predictable. When, let me be clear, *nothing* could be more predictable than the pathos ending of the Hero's Journey. He's going to die alone and regretful, is he? Shocking.

As a result of the above perceptions, the Heroine's Journey, when critically reviewed or discussed, tends to be perceived as smarmy, silly, frivolous, sappy, cheesy, predictable, tropey, effeminate, and weak. Of these, *tropey* is my least favorite criticism.

Both journeys are rife with tropes, but the fact that we criticize bastions of the Heroine's Journey for following predictable patterns (like romance) when those that follow the Hero's are given a pass (like most stories in the thriller genre) is beyond maddening.

Part of the reason for this critically negative gaze lies in the fact that our own culture is guilty of an overemphasis and glorification of the Hero's Journey. So gird your loins (heh heh) because I'm gonna talk about that next. We storytellers need to understand this because, when we write the Heroine's Journey, we are sending out a message with our narrative that is in direct conflict with prevailing social expectations.

2

HERO'S JOURNEY IN FOCUS

How we damage our own culture even more

The Hero's Journey emphasizes the following:

- individuality
- separation
- solo achievement over insurmountable odds
- revenge
- reticence in asking for help
- a savior or white knight complex
- success as defined by the death of another person

The Hero's Journey rarely contains comedy (if it does, it's usually snarky or dark humor or mockery). Romantic love or depictions of sex, if present, either act to seduce the hero away from his quest, or die in order to motivate the hero's revenge and spur him onward.

These stories are often described (positively) as gritty. Their endings will emphasize pathos and are usually lonely, bittersweet, tragic, or all three.

The Hero's Journey, when critically reviewed or discussed, is perceived as smart, realistic, exciting, heroic, noble, manly, and strong or powerful.

We writers often hear collective statements such as:

> "But we just *like* the Hero's Journey."

This happens at conferences, and at social gatherings with other writers or readers. Evidence presented in a previous segment in terms of sales and consumption would suggest the contrary, or at least that there is a hearty balance amongst buying readers. Even worse would be:

> "But the Hero's Journey is the *best* form of storytelling."

I was taught that in school, and have heard it parroted countless times since then. Now, that capitalizes on an insidious notion of *worthiness* and *value* that has been bestowed upon the Hero's Journey by both intentional and unintentional academic focus.

In the first case, more has been written about the Hero's Journey, and a great deal more time spent discussing it and intentionally activating it by pop culture, academics, critics, storytellers, and media. It's been given more attention. Glory, if you will.

In the second case, there's more to unpack in terms of the history of genre fiction and critics thereof, and I'll be going into that next.

3

REPERCUSSIONS OF BEING DEVALUED

Sex is NOT gender - the writer's ethical crutch

Let's return to that quote I do so love to analyze:

> "Women don't need to make the journey. In the whole mythological journey, the woman is there. All she has to do is realize that she's the place people are trying to get to."

Quite apart from everything else that is damaging about this statement, its wrongness comes not only from conflating gender with biological sex, but also from conflating biological sex with archetypes. And because of *that,* it's conflating personhood with male biological sex. I know that's a whole mess of *conflation* we've got going on, but I bring it up again now because this kind of culturewide assumptive association leads to the chronic, critical devaluation of the Heroine's Journey (and its genre representatives in the pop culture world).

Here's how...

Conflating biological sex with gender not only damages individuals, it profoundly corrupts social expectations of male and female on a massive scale.

These are core narrative journeys. They do more than just provide storytellers with story guides. They embed culturewide themes and messages.

This can make writers hesitant to tackle certain storylines, plot points, or scenes. It's an underpinning anxiety that can cause writer's block, without our even realizing it.

I want to emphasize that it is absolutely fine for writers or readers to prefer one journey over another, but when society performs a *moral* judgment on the *quality* of the Hero's Journey as superior to the Heroine's, this sends a damaging zeitgeist-wide *message* of preferential VALUE. Including how we, as writers, value our own work.

In other words, western society has intimately associated *hero* and masculine with what it means to be a *man* (and therefore what men are supposed to be and want in life) and simultaneously associated *heroine* and feminine with what it means to be a *woman* (and therefore what women are supposed to be and want in life). *Then* our society has decided that the first is morally better and ethically superior to the second.

Yeah, that's a blanket statement, but please think about it and how it might affect the way you write character and plot, and how you might be treated as a storyteller because of the kinds of characters and plots you scribble or prefer to consume.

The negative repercussions of how power and success are defined in these journeys sets up binary lifestyle expectations with staggering results, e.g., that a man's power is in solitary action, his success is in defeating someone else (usually another man) resulting in a white knight complex, while a woman's power (if it's even looked at outside of the context of the Hero's Journey) is nested in group action, and her success is in establishing family (defined as marriage or children) resulting in codependency and caregiver syndrome.

This is a direct result of neglecting to realize that these are gendered narratives.

Instead of seeing them as frameworks for story, we erroneously take them as guidelines for binary biological behavior within our own culture:

> The *hero* is what it *means* to be a *man*, or the *heroine* is what it *means* to be a *woman*.

With a binary biological sex application, fissions and divides begin to occur within culture, and the worst messages and themes possible from each journey are associated with linked biological sex characteristics.

Conversely, when the positives of each narrative are applied across all genders, something wonderful can occur, promoting both self-sufficiency and networking for strength in everyone.

By this I mean that if we look for a balance between the hero's strength in self-reliance plus the heroine's strength in delegating and asking for help, we can build not only well-rounded characters, but well-rounded and healthy careers as authors, and existences as humans.

Writers are the modern vanguards of narrative, and as such, we are in a dangerous position of power.

Promoting, writing, encouraging, and claiming that one journey is better than the other has tacitly conferred preferential *value* as a culture.

When we perform a moral or ethical judgment on the journey itself, touting one as superior to the other, especially unconsciously within an entire society, it sends a zeitgeist-wide message.

In this case that message is simple:

> The Hero's Journey is critically *worthy*, while the Heroine's Journey is not.

Stop this message.

What results is a wide-scale critical disregard for things like romantic comedies, romance novels, and so much more (despite the fact that they sell like hotcakes, so readers clearly want them).

Perhaps worse, this message disseminates an even more insidious idea:

> Anything built on the Heroine's Journey is weak, unworthy of attention, and inferior.

This will include your book, screenplay, movie, or your career when you chose this path, which, if the data at the beginning of this part tells you anything, suggests that this is patently untrue. Despite this chronic disenfranchisement, the Heroine's Journey keeps popping up in popular culture again and again. Readers want it, and readers buy it, no matter how much critics abuse it.

That is the tiny upside of this situation for writers.

Readers of the genres that embrace the Heroine's Journey also often feel attacked and abandoned and defensive (so they are on our side). They read the Heroine's Journey because they want the comfort and connection intrinsic to this narrative. Because this journey is about networking and cohesion, you will never find a more loyal group of readers. The author can become the heroine that readers have been looking for by writing the kinds of books they crave.

And with enough loyal readers, you have a career.

WHY DID THIS HAPPEN?

The persistent question

When I teach The Heroine's Journey as a seminar, one of the cries I always get at this juncture is...

Why?

Particularly from writers of romance who (let us be crystal clear here) have suffered horrible abuse from critics, fellow writers, and even readers and friends in the form of shaming, trolling, confrontation, online abuse, and anger. If you trot out that trite "but the writing is so bad in romance" at me, we will have *words*. There is just as much crap written in thrillers, science fiction, or any other commercial genre that features the hero as those that feature the heroine.

So, why?

Because the Heroine's Journey is a cornerstone of romance, cozy mysteries, comedy, and a great deal of fiction is targeted at, written by, and purchased by women and those who identify with a feminine-inclusive life experience.

ALSO, BLAME GOTHICS

So let's delve into them a little...

The disenfranchised nature of *all* genre fiction today is rooted in the Victorian critical attitude toward Gothic literature in England in the 1800s. The romance genre just happens to be fighting this battle on two fronts.

As authors, it's important to know how this happened and why, so we are better equipped to handle the consequences of these roots. Consequences that we cope with every day when writing this journey, in practice, online, and in real life.

HERE'S WHAT HAPPENED.

The rise of the middle class in England during the latter half of the Victorian era as a result of the industrial revolution included the passing of two Education Acts in 1870 and 1876 and, ultimately, the wide-scale education of women.

A rising middle class and increased urbanization brought with it shifting social structures as well.

Because of new mechanical technology, particularly those facilitating household tasks, and increased household income, these now literate women also had more leisure time and money to spend on it.

What did they do?

They purchased books and they read.

A lot.

Industrialization simultaneously provided for cheaper paper and defrayed printing costs, which resulted in the first incident (in the 1840s) of what we'd later call *pulp fiction*. The Victorians called these the *yellowbacks* and the *penny dreadfuls*.

Yellowbacks had bright inexpensive covers and were often smaller and lighter weight, making them ideal for rail travel, which by the mid to late 1800s was ubiquitous. Yellowbacks were poorly regarded as cheap products because of the way they were constructed, quite apart from their content. The cheapness of the packaging soon became conflated with the quality of content and story within.

Just prior to the rise of yellowbacks came the rise of the Romantic Gothics, spearheaded by the acclaimed authoress and purveyor of melodramatic sensibility, Ann Radcliffe (whose books were described by her, and critics, as *romances*). Her novel *The Mysteries of Udolpho* (1794), was a massive bestseller, and started a trend that would persist throughout the Victorian era, encompassing the yellowbacks.

One side effect of Radcliffe's books was a movement of derivative romances (in the Gothic sense of the term, see upcoming section) predominantly written by and for women.

While Radcliffe was generally well regarded during her day, her Gothic-writing followers were considered poor imitations and proponents of sensationalist women's entertainment. Radcliffe was tainted by association and generally neglected by twentieth-century critics and literary historians (Rogers 1994). Ian Watt, for example, barely mentions Radcliffe, or any women authors, in his 1957 *Rise of the Novel.* An anonymous critic in *Time* magazine in 1966 called Radcliffe one of the "ickiest prigs who ever put quill to paper" (Rogers 1994, p. 88).

The most critically abused scion of Radcliffe was Marie Corelli, who wrote (starting in 1886) a mix of romance, occultism, mystery, and Christian morality. Sales of her novels exceeded the combined sales of her male author compatriots: Arthur Conan Doyle, H. G. Wells, and Rudyard Kipling! Corelli was globally popular, much beloved by readers, and roundly abused by critics as melodramatic and plebeian. *The Spectator* said she was "accepted as a genius by a public to whose commonplace sentimentalities and prejudices she gave a glamorous setting" (Scott 1955, 30). One cannot help but note a certain parallel to *Twilight*, can one?

So what we have, then, is a conflation of events during the second half of the Victorian era:

1. the rise of a popular Gothic-born genre
2. written and read by women
3. produced cheaply in mass quantities
4. roundly vilified by bastions of literature, male

     critics, and self-proclaimed proponents of good
     taste for all three reasons

Thus, when someone criticizes romance, I love to clap slowly and praise them for participating in two hundred years of misogyny.

Despite this, the commercial genres, dominated by science fiction, fantasy, crime fiction, and romance (which all owe most of their tropes and archetypes to these very Gothics) are *the most* read of all fiction.

The Gothics spawned westerns (AKA Old West adventure novels), historical fiction, mysteries, thrillers and crime fiction, horror, fantasy, science fiction, romance, and now YA (which includes elements of many of the above and is a modern marketing bracket).

A cultural disregard of the Heroine's Journey, combined with critical distaste for commercial genre fiction as a result of its Gothic heritage, has put romance in particular on the embattled list. But don't forget how science fiction and mysteries were once there too, during the age of the pulps.

These days, it certainly feels like we must defend our right to write romance or to read it, as romance is often called out in the popular press for being tropey, sappy, immature, or lowbrow. It is one of the few genres remaining where culture demands that those of us who enjoy romance justify this preference, whether as readers or writers. As romance is conflated with (and dependent upon) the Heroine's Journey, this has also caused it to be (when talked of at all) equally devalued.

CHAPTER 7: GENRE COMPLICATIONS

How the Gothics impact narrative

Now that I've addressed how the advent of the Gothics further helped to disenfranchise the Heroine's Journey and commercial genre fiction, I'd like to discuss how the Gothics also impacted the narrative nature of both journeys, in ways that writers and readers can benefit from understanding.

This should help you tap into the tropes to better enhance the expectation and experience of your Heroine's Journey, and guide you in the use of archetypes to surprise your audience with new twists on old characters.

WHY GOTHIC LITERATURE?

Why do we need to know about the Gothics, aside from the fact that they are the main reason genres like science fiction, fantasy, and romance are disregarded by critics?

Because while a lot of narrative structure, core themes, and plot beats are sourced in the Hero's and the Heroine's Journeys, a number of our tropes and archetypes come from the Gothics.

> If the Heroine's Journey is our foundation, then Gothic tropes and archetypes are our building blocks.

These help us construct the vital supporting cast of characters for our heroine and also influence our reader's emotional journey.

It's actually really cool stuff. You see, the combination of how we manipulate the journey and how we have evolved the Gothic elements pretty much allows us to hack what the reader needs from most major commercial genres... and the resulting messages we authors leave behind.

A BIT OF GOTHIC HISTORY

Horace Walpole's *The Castle of Otranto* (1764) is generally regarded as the first true Gothic romance. Many of the early Gothics immediately following this book were thinly disguised religious diatribes against the seductive nature of the devil (like Matthew Lewis's *The Monk* 1796).

Later, via Radcliffe, the yellowbacks, and beyond, we begin to see books like Mary Shelley's *Frankenstein* or Robert Louis Stevenson's *The Strange Case of Dr Jekyll and Mr Hyde,* both of which (partly because of the industrial revolution) explore themes of technology as both savior and destroyer.

This shifted Gothic narratives away from religious themes toward the idea that evil is manifested as mankind's own hubristic reliance on scientific discovery and academic intellect – themes that are still revisited in science fiction today. Incidentally, Radcliffe forms a kind of bridge, as it was she who developed the Scooby-Doo technique, where every seemingly supernatural intrusion is eventually traced back to natural causes.

The Gothic movement spawned most of what we think of today as commercial genre fiction, from mystery to romance, from science fiction to fantasy, from thriller to horror, whether Heroine's Journey or Hero's Journey.

It's worth looking a little closer at the archetypes and tropes that typify the Gothics and how these impacted the narrative elements of the two journeys, because it is a combination of the three that has resulted in the most popular fiction written and consumed today.

1

GOTHIC ARCHETYPES & THE HEROINE

It's all about sex and gender (isn't everything?)

The most common archetypes in Gothic literature are as follows.

GOTHIC ARCHETYPES

Human Eve

Our heroine, is destined to survive the story, learn the appropriate life lessons, and probably marry the hero.

Innocent Eve

Usually Human Eve's sister or friend, is a tragic heroine destined to succumb or die (precious cinnamon roll, too pure for this world).

Evil Eve

Our sorceress, seductress, or bad queen, is a power-hungry mistress of manipulation who will either descend into madness or in some way destroy herself with ambition.

The Hero

A manly man, will rescue Human Eve and save the day through destruction of a Villain.

The Villain

A corrupt and abusive tyrant, often a thinly disguised (or actual) sexual predator, is after our Human Eve (or both Eves) and represents all that is dangerous to an untried young lady of quality. He often showcases everything that can be bad about a hero from a Hero's Journey, which is to say, he holds a great deal of power over others, doesn't fit into civilized life, is temperamental and violent, and when we encounter him, he is (and should remain) alone.

GOTHIC ARCHETYPES IN ACTION: DANGEROUS LIAISONS

An excellent example of a classic Gothic melodrama featuring every single one of the above-named archetypes (and a few of the more minor ones as well, like the wise servant) is the 1988 movie *Dangerous Liaisons*. Here we see Uma Thurman's Cécile de Volanges as Human Eve, Michelle Pfeiffer's Madame de Tourvel as Innocent Eve, Glenn Close's Marquise de Merteuil as Evil Eve, Keanu Reeves's Chevalier Danceny as the Hero, and John Malkovich's Vicomte de Valmont as the Villain.

Each representative archetype in this movie remains true to their role in any classic Gothic work. Essentially the plot is as follows.

Evil Eve arranges the disgrace of Human Eve for revenge, by getting the Villain to seduce her. At first he declines because he is already attempting to seduce famously pious Innocent Eve. Evil Eve ups the ante: If he can deflower

Innocent Eve, Evil Eve will sleep with him as a reward. Full of hubris and unable to refuse a challenge, the Villain accepts.

Meanwhile, Human Eve meets the Hero. They fall in love, coaxed by Evil Eve because the Hero is a commoner, and his love will also ruin Human Eve.

Meanwhile, the Villain successfully seduces Innocent Eve, but uh-oh, also falls in love with her. Evil Eve mocks his love, which humiliates him into breaking up with Innocent Eve.

Innocent Eve's grief and shame result in illness. Guilt-ridden, the Villain lashes out at Evil Eve. She responds by exposing his tryst with Human Eve to the Hero.

The Hero challenges the Villain to a duel. The Villain loses and pushes himself onto the blade in a kind of suicide. Dying, he asks the Hero to tell Innocent Eve of his love for her, and his death. The Hero does this and then Innocent Eve also dies.

The Villain has given the Hero Evil Eve's letters, which expose her for the evil she is. The Hero disseminates the letters to high society, destroying Evil Eve and turning her into a social pariah. Her punishment is removal of all connections and the ability to manipulate the people around her (the seat of her power).

I know, messy, but if you really want details, just watch the movie. It's excellent.

As I hope you can see, the plot of the movie emphasizes Gothic archetypes in the story arc of each character. From motivation to the death of the Villain at the Hero's hand to the fact that Innocent Eve literally pines away, to the destruction of Evil Eve being one of humiliation rather than physical suffering... all of these are Gothic standards.

THE BYRONIC HERO

In some cases, the two Gothic masculine archetypes of Hero and Villain are combined into the wildly popular, tortured Byronic Hero (of which, incidentally, Marvel's *Wolverine* is an excellent example). Byronic Heroes, like Gothic Villains, tend to be cunning and rather ruthless, as well as arrogant and prone to violence. However, as they are also self-aware, they yield easily to depression, usually because of the state of their own moral turpitude, and are therefore emotionally and intellectually tortured.

A fascinating archetype, the Byronic Hero remains extremely appealing to modern audiences (everyone loves a bad boy). In his original Gothic form, he's a true Hero's Journey hero, in that he cannot be redeemed through the love of a good woman – often because he chooses to love someone else's wife – but is entirely self-destructive and will end up in bittersweet pathos. Our Byronic Hero is usually *made into the difficult yet lovable man he is* through a malfunction of family or a problematic childhood (I'm looking at you, Batman).

If we inject the Byronic Hero into a Heroine's Journey, he can be saved though love and connection and a new family unit.

Or, if you inject him into a Hero's Journey and redeem him before self-sacrifice, he will tear the heartstrings of your readers.

For a writer, either route you take with a Byronic Hero, makes for an extremely appealing character, partly because of the history we have as a culture with this archetype.

The romance genre has interceded on the Byronic Hero's behalf and upended this archetype's original path by imposing the Heroine's Journey upon him so that the love of the *right* woman is the only thing that can now save him. Edward in *The Twilight Saga* is an excellent example of this archetype. Since the Heroine's Journey is all about solidarity, a heroine can rescue the Byronic Hero through the application of family networking (sex, love, or give that dude a baby), because the end goal is her connection with him, not his own connection to, or following of, a Hero's Journey path. She has successfully diverted him from his inevitable doom had he been on a Hero's Journey and not part of her story.

The salvation of the troubled alpha male is an incredibly popular trope, and in many ways can be seen as the Heroine's Journey interceding with and diverting the expected narrative beats of the Hero's Journey. If allowed to continue his journey, an alpha male character ends up victorious but alone.

However, if he has entered the purview of a heroine's book (as the redeemable bad boy of a romance novel, for example, or perhaps a lovable trickster) he is now part of a Heroine's Journey, and she *will* save him by pulling all his pieces back together, giving him family to love, and teaching him the art of compromise. (And possibly procreating with his faux cock in order to provide for a continuation of the cycle of life... Isis, I'm looking at you.)

In other words, I find it easy to understand why the *save the alpha-hole with love* concept is so powerful, particularly in romance. It represents the tacit victory of a Heroine's Journey over a Hero's. This is also why it's so threatening to critics. I bet this discussion made you wince, right? Well, it did if you're not a romance writer.

Nevertheless, the irrepressible, snarky, alpha bad boy with a ton of sex appeal and physical prowess is practically ubiquitous in modern iterations of both the Heroine's and the Hero's Journeys. He can impact the resonance and power of any narrative, not to mention provide audiences with a particularly appealing character.

THE GOTHIC JOURNEY

You can see, I hope, how the beats of the Heroine's Journey might complement or conflict with any one of the Gothic archetypes I listed above.

If you're going to employ an Evil Eve archetype, for example, within a Hero's Journey, her role will be to stagnate him with seduction. However, if you want to put her into a Heroine's Journey, she will try to separate the heroine from her family and increase character isolation. Our Evil Eve can fulfill her destiny of insanity or self-destruction in either narrative, but in the Hero's Journey she's more likely to die, whereas in the Heroine's Journey she's more likely to descend into ignominy or madness.

In fact, because these archetypes are so endemic to genre, as storytellers our twisting, gender bending, and making use of any of them will tap into audience expectations and allow for manipulation of readers regardless of narrative journey. I believe in being aware of these undercurrents with the characters. Use them if you dare.

I had great fun subverting the Byronic character archetype in *Soulless*, by making my alpha hero literally the alpha of a werewolf pack, and then subverting him by making him very family oriented, bewildered by his burgeoning affection, and overly emotional in his need to connect and communicate.

I could do all of this, and get a very likable character out the other end, because I knew the original archetype that I was playing against.

GOTHIC TROPES & THE HEROINE

World building meets commercial genre fiction

Gothic literature is littered with tropes as well as archetypes, and as predictable as a modern audience now finds many of these, the fact remains that genre writers often rely upon them as cornerstones of our story setting, atmosphere, and structure.

They are still used, over and over again.

Tropes are a kind of shorthand to communicate possible outcomes to readers, and to control their expectations of our story's plot. Then we can either surprise them with a twist away from these expectations by breaking with the trope, or satisfy them and make them feel clever for having intrinsically understood the inevitable outcome. Satisfaction and surprise are two of our best tools as authors.

Knowing how a trope interacts with and impacts a Hero's or Heroine's Journey can help you overcome writer's block, move your characters forward toward success and change, and also help you better promote and understand where your final story fits in the market and how it can honor reader expectations and build a loyal fan base.

SETTING AS CHARACTER

First of all, the Gothics exemplified setting as character and this trope persists into noir, horror, science fiction, fantasy, small-town cozies, and many more subsets of commercial genre fiction. Any genre book where the removal of the world building would result in a complete loss of story or plot is employing this Gothic trope. Noir is a near perfect example, where the city setting is almost as important as the main character.

In fact, I would go so far as to say there are some critics who believe that if the setting isn't character, if it's only there as a *trapping* or *set dressing* that could easily be removed without destroying the story, than that book hasn't earned the *right* to that genre's moniker.

Sci-fi romance gets this a lot. If readers criticize a book for being too much romance and not enough science fiction, they are often responding to a lack of sufficient setting. Incidentally, you can solve this by making the science an integral part of the romance thread, having the hero be part cyborg, for example, and believing himself unworthy of love as a result.

Using setting as character, making the surroundings a part of the story, pushes your book more thoroughly into its genre or subgenre. This will make it more marketable, among other things.

ATMOSPHERE OF MYSTERY

The idea that there is something to be found out, something mysterious, about the setting or the characters is a trope that has bled into most modern genre fiction.

Most science fiction operates on some level as an exploration of a technological mystery and its impact on the world around the characters, just as most fantasy touches on the evolution and exploration of a magical system, one that your readers learn more about alongside the characters. Even horror often delves into the why of the paranormal presence.

Then there's the whole mystery genre, not to mention romantic suspense and thrillers. There may be no actual mystery in your book, but in many subsets of genre fiction, there is likely to be some level of mysterious atmosphere.

Adding an aura of mystery or sense of wonder to your world building, and having the reader and character discover more about the world together, gives readers an additional reason to keep reading. Not only will they want to find out what happens next to the characters, they want to find out more about the world you've built, and how that world will be impacted and changed by your characters.

A PROPHECY

Most Gothic novels involved a prophecy of some kind. These days, we often see this trope in genres that deal with the supernatural – fantasy, superheroes, and YA in particular, but it also taps into the Hero's or Heroine's

Journey tropes of unique abilities, powers, godlike tendencies, or fated birth.

It can creep into all commercial genres under the guise of *specialness*, particularly key to the Hero's Journey, but also present for the goddess heroine and her ability to disguise her true nature and divinity.

We can also think of the prophecy as the confluence of a particular set of skills (acquired, learned, or self-taught) that distinguishes our hero or heroine as *better* than other humans. Viewing it in that light allows us to spot this trope all over, from Sherlock Holmes to Batman to Katniss Everdeen.

The prophecy of specialness trope may be overused, but it has enduring appeal. Harry Potter is an excellent example.

How a character copes with being special is great meat for writers and readers – whether they can avoid their fate or embrace it. This is particularly true in YA, because every teen wants to be special.

This trope may be tired, but it will not sleep. Use it and the critics might hate you, and the older readers who have seen it a million times before might get annoyed with you, but new readers, younger readers, will fall in love with your main character and you might just have the next runaway hit on your hands.

OMENS AND SUPERNATURAL ELEMENTS

Gothic literature was replete with portents, visions, and spooky dreams – a trope that these days is most often seen in the form of foreshadowing. It's going to be most common in those genres that also maintain Gothic literature's supernatural connection, like fantasy, horror, urban fantasy, paranormal romance, and associated YA.

A recent example is the witch Melisandre in *Game of Thrones* (2011), who brings many visions and messages from her god to the people of Westeros. The characters of Alice in *The Twilight Saga* or Sybill Trelawney in the Harry Potter series represent Gothic seers relaying portentous omens.

OVERWROUGHT EMOTION

Sentimentality was a hallmark of the Gothics. A reliance on, and systemic use of, emotions and feelings of intimacy to drive the story is now the provenance of those brands of genre fiction that also employ the Heroine's Journey... cozy mystery, romance, space opera, political fantasy, and YA.

I'd caution against conflating this kind of intimacy with stories that use sexual relationships, rape, and incest as plot devices, like *Game of Thrones* (2011), since it's not the same thing (see earlier discussions on a heroine's motivation). Although, to be fair, both are variations on this particular trope.

Rape, for example, is an act of violence, not intimacy. It is an act that isolates a heroine and will make her feel more alone. If it must appear in your book, one way to correct for it and bring yourself back to a Heroine's Journey is to build your heroine a female friendship network who gather about her and support her through her resulting crisis. But I don't recommend its use.

When writing a Heroine's Journey, you'll likely adapt the *overwrought emotion* trope into employing these emotions as a means of connection between characters, usually through dialogue or physical intimacy, or both, at significant pivotal plot points in the story.

In other words, your main character is best able to change her mind, change her movement through space and time, or change her feelings about someone or something because of conversation, sex, or intimacy.

If you are at a crossroads, stagnated, or facing writer's block, and you're writing a Heroine's Journey?

Introduce a new character or bring back an old one who has an emotional interaction with your main character, and see if that shakes things up a bit.

DAMSEL IN DISTRESS

There's a lot of wailing women in white robes being rescued at the last minute from the clutch of a sexually lustful villain in the Gothics. You're wincing, I know, but this trope *will not die.*

The biological sex of those wailing isn't always female anymore, but this one is still around. Our hero sure does like to rescue damsels, even though that damsel will eventually try to waylay or trap him into abandoning his quest. And our heroine is practically compelled to rescue anyone in distress, as a prospective new networking opportunity.

We will continue to write this trope. I simply urge you to make very careful choices about the nature of the distress (does it *have* to be sexual?) and the gender, race, and sexual identity of your damsel.

The damsel trope is a profoundly powerful representation of weakness. We authors must be *wary of who appears weak or victimized* in our books, as the message this sends can detrimentally impact an audience's sense of self-worth.

RIVAL LOVERS

This is awfully common in Gothic literature, where usually the romantic Hero and the Villain archetypes are vying for Human Eve's attention. This has morphed into the love triangle that experiences spates of being wildly popular and is particularly common in fantasy, romance, and YA. See *Twilight* or *To All the Boys I've Loved Before* (2014).

Often this is simply a vehicle for showcasing the desirability of the heroine. It is pretty rare (though not unheard of) for rivals to come to blows in a Heroine's Journey, since she is motivated to work with other characters, not pit them against each other. Unless, of course, you're writing an Evil Eve style antiheroine, in which case she will network for manipulation and her favorite tool is an alpha type that she can finagle into taking on all comers.

We see the Rival Lovers trope pop up in the Hero's Journey, often to push the hero into a jealous rage and get him to kill people. This version of the trope is likely born out of Shakespeare and fairy tales.

The rival lovers trope can be fun to employ and fun to subvert.

I used it myself in my Parasol Protectorate series to have background dialogue with my readers on the nature of monogamy and bisexuality. I introduced a female cross-dressing character as a love interest to my heroine, as a means of playing with the complex nature of the love triangle. This also tested reader expectations concerning my main character's sexual orientation, as well as that character's loyalty and continued interest in her werewolf love interest. This added *Will she? Won't she?* moments of tension.

Because readers expected one kind of love triangle – two boys and a girl – making it a boy, a girl, and a cross-dressing French inventor allowed me to reveal a great deal more about all three of those characters and opened up possible futures to tempt readers into turning the next page.

METONYMY

Pretty rare these days, I mention this last Gothic trope because I happen to find it fascinating (and it's a *great* word to trot out at cocktail parties).

> Also, it's super dangerous for storytellers to use metonymy without realizing it.

Most commonly found in horror, noir, science fiction, and fantasy, and partly sourced in fairy stories, metonymy is a subtype of metaphor in which something (like rain or the color blue) is used to stand for something else (like sorrow).

Metonymy is partly responsible for the more insidious idea that a corrupt personality manifests in appearance, i.e., that *evil* means *ugly* or *fat*.

As storytellers, this is another trope we must be particularly careful not to activate unconsciously, because it perpetuates a damaging message of aesthetic intolerance.

Just as we should be careful about whom we make weak in our stories, we must be particularly wary of in whom and how villainy appears, in terms of appearance, gender, disability, neurodiversity, sexuality, and race.

Before you claim that you need to be "true to yourself and your story," please check to make sure you aren't instead falling prey to a lifetime of fairy stories and their insidious metonymy.

> The message perpetuated by utilizing this trope can be profoundly damaging, both to the world and to your career.

On a different note, the most common use of metonymy now is actually in cover art design.

For example, the way an urban fantasy cover is usually in blues and purples (sadness, angst) with a solitary shadow figure and a cityscape background. Or the way contemporary romance often uses bright, cheerful, rosy color palettes (passion and femininity) and swirly calligraphic type (to be blamed on the Victorians and their Valentine's cards).

Color choices, figure placement (if there is a figure), lettering, and so forth not only convey genre to the readers, but also mood and emotional content – metonymy.

GOTHIC LIT AND THE HEROINE'S JOURNEY

Since the Gothics source some of their archetypes and tropes in fairy tales and some in the works of Shakespeare and his contemporaries, a clean application of the narrative beats onto or into the Heroine's Journey is challenging. A writer will want to use them because they can set up reader expectations, which can then be subverted, adding elements of surprise and excitement.

A new twist on an old trope will charm jaded readers and a revisit of an expected trope treated with delicacy can leave them feeling satisfied that they guessed what might happen. It's a fun line to tread – a touch of surprise balanced by a touch of expectation – but it will leave your readers feeling happy and satisfied.

How does this tie back to the Heroine's Journey?

Well, readers of this journey want to be left with a feeling of satisfaction and comfort. Using the tropes of the genre you are writing can certainly help with that.

The influence of Gothic literature on commercial genre fiction means it's difficult to write a beat-by-beat version of either journey that also cleanly fits into modern genre fiction, but that's why we have these tropes and archetypes as touchstones.

This is one of the many reasons I speak of both journeys as narrative *guides*, not firm dictates, since if you're going to write commercial genre fiction, your characters will likely include various iterations of the source journey *and* somewhat incompatible Gothic archetypes and tropes. But if you can balance these things, your books appeal on multiple levels, both the core that the journeys provide, and the emotional touchstones that the Gothics enforced.

GOTHIC SIDE EFFECTS

Some interesting repercussions

I wasn't sure exactly where to put this section, but I didn't want to leave it out, as it's particularly relevant to those who write contemporary romance (the most popular kind of romance by a long shot), modern thrillers, and (some) literary fiction or memoir. (Are you a memoirist? Hello, oh peculiar stranger reading this tome.)

Your access to and use of Gothic tropes and archetypes is likely to be different.

In fact, I like to argue that one of the reasons behind the extraordinary success of contemporary romance in particular (and its popularity as the bestselling and most read subgenre of commercial fiction) is that the story works best in what one might call a *white box*.

That's not meant as an insult.

It means that the characters could easily exist outside of time and place, yet the story would still work. These kinds of books tend to be dialogue (Heroine's Journey) and/or action (Hero's Journey) heavy – these can manifest in violence or sex/romance.

In other words, a good, well-told thriller just as much as a sweet contemporary romance might be lifted out and put into any setting. Writers of mystery can and do tinker with this, by leaning toward noir with an emphasis on setting, but the heavy hitters (pun intended) are usually exciting and heart palpitating regardless of anything beyond action, reaction, and character interaction. Another way to put this is:

> The characters could exist inside a white box.

Nora Roberts's contemporary romance novels are excellent examples of this. From a storyteller's perspective, writing this kind of narrative is a highly marketable skill.

If you want to churn out books, you can make minor tweaks and keep writing essentially the same book over and over again, because it has little dependency on many of the tropes I just talked about. Fantasy, science fiction, and noir are hobbled by one of the very things that defines them – setting as character. Both the relationship and the adventure will have to pause on occasion to describe the universe. There are readers who yearn for that exact thing – a richly built world and a break in which to appreciate it – but then there are *also* those who prefer a white box where the pacing is fast and the setting practically irrelevant.

I sometimes think that some of the true cross-genres, like sci-fi romance, struggle the most because the dominant readership in romance is after a white box book, whereas the dominant readership in science fiction is looking for descriptions of technology and science. It's challenging, not necessarily to write something like sci-fi romance (because they are both still rooted in the Gothics), but to find a big enough audience of readers who will embrace something like sci-fi romance. Each side has been trained into following subgenres away from diametrically opposed tropes and stylings.

I mention this merely because it's a matter of personal taste, but also a matter of where the genres we write within have migrated. Theoretically, for writers, any genre could be any journey, but the devoted readers within a specific genre have certain expectations. Those expectations are not *just* of these archetypes and tropes, and which ones are still utilized or emphasized the most, but of which Journey the chassis of your narrative is built upon.

In other words, yes, you can write a Heroine's Journey thriller, but either you're going to find your reader base profoundly disappointed in you, or you'll end up writing Romantic Suspense instead (and that's okay, I promise).

A JOURNEY TO MARKET

As you write your story, it behooves you to think through audience expectations as part of your writing process when you are deciding what tropes to use and which journey your main character is undertaking.

You might find yourself shifting journeys in order to accommodate your audience. That's okay, because the journey is there to help you, not hinder you, and your book will be stronger for finding its niche and focus.

These inclinations and associations are not set in stone.

Some highly successful books break the models (and literary fiction usually ignores them entirely), but it behooves us to be aware of how the journeys have been affected by the Gothics, and how this in turn affects reader expectations so that we gain control over our own narratives and, eventually, where they sit in the market.

> The last thing any writer needs or wants is a bunch of readers who feel betrayed by a story, and leave bad reviews because of it.

Your aforementioned thriller reader looking for a Hero's Journey might feel, for example, that you (the author) have heartlessly tricked them into reading romantic suspense, because that's usually a Heroine's Journey.

And heaven forfend you pitch to the romantic suspense audience and what you've written is actually a thriller where, in classic hero fashion, he wins the day but loses the girl in the final shootout. Because very little in this market is less forgiving than a romance reader who was not warned about a cliffhanger or who did not get their happy ending.

> Because the Heroine's Journey promises comfort, reader expectations for the heroine are easily crushed.

The sense of betrayal is greater if you promise affection and deliver hurt, than vice versa. Believe me, your readers will feel very betrayed.

Deciding which tropes to employ and which journey to use greatly impacts the reader experience and what audience your book will appeal to. It's better to do this consciously than unconsciously.

Your role, then, as a storyteller (should you choose to accept it), is to pick and choose which elements work best for *your* fictional work, from archetypes, to tropes, to journeys.

It might help us to look closely at what narrative beats of the Heroine's Journey resonate *now* with modern audiences (and how they've evolved), especially given the post-Gothic space in which we find ourselves as writers.

So, when you next experience a popular movie or book, you might come back to this part or revisit the beats of the two journeys, and try to understand what has been used successfully and why it works.

CHAPTER 8: NARRATIVE VARIATIONS

Complexity and young adult stories

In order to reinforce the fact that there's a great deal more complexity to these narratives than is evident at first, this part is going to delve into some of the most common variations and applications of the different journeys, as well as what happens when they are combined and how they can be manipulated to engender an emotional response in readers.

These are fun to write, but it's better to activate them thoughtfully, because readers will become more invested if you know how to manipulate emotions with these characters.

YA STORIES

But first, a word on young adult narratives featuring coming-of-age narratives.

YA stories can utilize either journey with great success.

A YA book or teen movie/TV show may tackle the evolution from teen to adult in terms of learning autonomy, self-sufficiency, loneliness coping strategies, sacred duty, solo responsibility, and fortitude. Or it may tackle it in terms of learning one's place in society, belonging, forming friendship groups and experiencing love, developing better communication skills, and discovering leadership abilities. In the first case, your teen is becoming a hero, in the second a heroine.

TRAGIC JOURNEYS

Let's just make everyone cry, okay?

The tragic take on these two narratives is certainly worth exploring, if you're the kind of storyteller who wants people to cry.

TRAGIC HERO'S JOURNEY

As a general rule, the hero is killed by his own hubris in pursuit of power or glory; occasionally he can be called upon to sacrifice himself for others, but sacrifice works best if he is doing it for a concept or an ideal.

His journey is by its very nature a little tragic. He usually cannot return to the civilization he is trying to save, because he has become too powerful or too lost on his quest. Also, as civilization is correlated with femininity and stasis, our hero will lose what it means to *be* a hero if he returns and reintegrates fully into cohesive society.

I call these *extreme heroes*. Heracles is a great example of a hero who grew so heroic there was no way he could ever return home.

The extreme hero is destined to die, while the regular hero ends up alone, voluntarily or involuntarily. Pop culture examples include Luke Skywalker of the *Star Wars* franchise, and Jon Snow of the *Game of Thrones* television series (2011).

TRAGIC HEROINE'S JOURNEY

On the flip side, the tragic heroine almost always sacrifices herself for the greater good of a society, or for her friends and family so that they may live on together in harmony.

Interestingly, a heroine corrupted by a lust for power (which is more commonly a hero's choice) is often driven into madness – good examples of this being the archetypal evil fairytale queen, or characters like Lady Macbeth.

Now, once again, I'm going to remind you that these two journeys are chassis, not outlines. Not every modern version of the journey will fit every point of its associated narrative. Also, not every modern story *should* necessarily fit entirely into one or the other.

This is a case of training your pattern recognition as a writer, but not forcing yourself to accommodate the model against your ingrained instincts. Knowing the two journeys and what makes them different should help you write, not hinder you from telling the story you really want or need to tell.

With that in mind, let's talk about exceptions, variations, and ways writers might manipulate these two narratives.

ADDITIONAL NARRATIVE ELEMENTS

More archetypes, tropes, and themes

In this section, I'm going into a few other things writers might need to consider that didn't fit comfortably anywhere else in this book.

A VERY PARTICULAR SET OF SKILLS

The idea of singular specialness (*prophecy*) comes to genre fiction from the Gothics and shows up in both journeys with the main character manifesting unique abilities.

If you are writing a hero, his abilities will probably be offensive, as his skill set rests in dealing out death (pointy objects and things that go *bang* are preferred).

If you're writing a heroine, her abilities should probably be defensive, as her skill set rests in shielding and protection (although she will also make a pretty solid inventor).

As I have said before, no one could have been more pleased than I when Bella in *The Twilight Saga* got her vampire special ability in the final book and what was it?

Shielding! Nothing could possibly be more Heroine's Journey than that. Way to hit a trope out of the park.

I can't let the concept of prophecy go by without mentioning another endemic archetype of genre fiction, exemplified by the flighty yet well-meaning Divination teacher, Sybill Trelawney, in the Harry Potter franchise, and that is...

THE MAD PROPHET & THE WISE FOOL

If you want to go way back into the misty roots of western mythos, one might first peg Kassandra as the birth of this archetype – the mad prophetess, she who was destined to speak the truth and yet never to be believed. Probably tied to the Oracle at Delphi, who was supposed to do the Ancient Greek equivalent of inhaling hallucinogenic smoke, speaking in tongues, and telling the future (as you do).

The idea of a (usually gendered feminine or sexless) side character who dreams and has visions of the future is one picked up, and put down, and fooled around with in many different genres – from the mercurial Doctor Who, to various superheroes, to the aforementioned Alice in *The Twilight Saga*.

There are spinoff historical iterations of this archetype as well, such as the wise slave (particularly in Roman comedies), or the wise fool (hellooo Shakespeare), the noble jester, or the wise servant (I'm looking at you, Jeeves). There's a near constant rehash of the crazy, lowly, or ill-educated character whom one expects to be ignorant of all things important but instead knows all, or at least knows vital secret things, usually about the future.

There's a fine line between the form this archetype takes, and the genre and tenor of the book in which it appears, not just the journey they're assisting (and they are always trying to provide an assist). In comedy, the wise fool eventually convinces the main character to the benefit of all, or at least the benefit of the main character.

In tragedy, the prophet is ignored and Troy falls.

Incidentally, Sybill Trelawney is a very clever name, as prophetic women in the Graeco-Roman world were often called Sibyls.

HOW DOES THIS ARCHETYPE INTERSECT WITH THE HEROINE?

Heroines make friends and allies of the prophet/wise fool characters. Heroes ignore or dismiss them, usually for hubristic reasons. This archetype is a crowd pleaser when applied judiciously within the context of teams, capers, buddy cop, police procedural, multiple POV, comedy and (specifically) the Heroine's Journey.

In fact, this character can become one of the most appealing to your readers, carrying tremendous audience appeal. Also, they are pretty useful for info-dumping. I'm thinking, of course, of such characters as Spock from *Star Trek: The Original Series* (1966), Data from *Star Trek: The Next Generation* (1987), or Brainy when he crosses into the *Supergirl* TV show (2015).

On the flip side, this archetype can also go badly astray: for example, Jar Jar Binks in the second round offering of the *Star Wars* franchise (1999–2005).

This character can be (and often is) a fish-out-of-water prophet. Aliens to the culture in which they find themselves, be it extraterrestrial or international aliens. They can function as foils for your main character, and in doing so, expose more information to readers about both the main character and the world that character comfortably inhabits (which the alien does not).

They are also great comic relief... enter Iambe, may she tell ribald jokes and make Demeter smile.

A hero is destined never to believe the prophet or the good advice (or perhaps just not take the alien seriously). In fact, the ancient Greeks often punished their heroes for not taking an oracle's warning to heart, for trying to avoid fate, or for doing the right thing for the wrong reason.

But a heroine can believe the prophetess. She will probably befriend her and make good use of her abilities. In *The Twilight Saga,* Alice provides the vehicle and means for a negotiated reunification at the end of the series, preventing massive death and destruction. Alice returns having undertaken her own search to retrieve evidence that supports Bella – that allows for the continuation of Bella's newly established familial network.

I should add that there is an inclination to use children (gendered sexless by narrative) in the prophet/wise fool role (see *Dune* and its subsequent franchise). The sagacious precocious child becomes an instrument of guidance to adult characters, and a plot device that encourages characters to both protect and learn. Plus, there is something simultaneously twisted and appealing in the notion of a child directing adult action, a power play that can be turned creepy by the horror genre or made adorable with a lighter touch (see the precocious child in sitcoms or romances).

Of course, how this child is perceived is also a marker of which narrative they occupy. Alia Atreides in *Dune* is, in fact, a doomed prophetess, her very existence a herald of evil for both the hero and his enemy. *Star Trek: The Next Generation*'s child genius Wesley Crusher (1987) could just as easily appear in *Children of the Corn* (1977), but as he's hanging out in a kindly space opera Heroine's Journey, so he's gonna be fine. (Although, beating the archetype on the head, they promptly put him in charge of driving the ship. Literally, he's the guide and navigator. Of course he is. Prophet allegory much?)

DEUS EX HELPER

A main character saved by the intervention of outside supernatural elements, or even just friends or family, can anger a modern audience. I'll never forget listening to a dude on a podcast (as you do) complaining bitterly about the fact that every time Harry Potter went to confront Voldemort, he just had to have a visit from dead family members first. But for a heroine, receiving assistance is not a weakness. It is a strength. Harry *can't* go it alone, because he's a heroine, and he needs his family.

Still, if you're writing the Heroine's Journey, you're likely to come up against this kind of criticism. I tend to shrug and carry on; after all, it appears to have worked out fine for J. K. Rowling despite that dude's complaining on the podcast.

If you're worried, a focus on ensuring that the assistance of friends and family appears *necessary* (the military general approach – activate strengths in others to cover apparent weaknesses in the self) should keep this criticism in check. Concentrate on the value that the assistive side character provides to the success of the journey, rather than on the heroine's need.

In other words, it's not that the heroine isn't good at casting fireballs, it's that she knows her BFF is better, and so she may have to put that BFF at risk in order to best deploy fireballs. This will also cause readers to value those side characters in their own right, and will them to succeed as much as the heroine.

GROUP DYNAMICS

Another difference between the two narratives that I feel is important for storytellers to understand because it will help create emotional depth and motivation in your story, is *how* the heroine or the hero approaches a group.

For our hero, groups and crowds represent the threat of war, the stagnation of civilization, or the possibility of betrayal. Our hero is most likely to think:

> I *can't* trust others.

For our heroine, groups and crowds represent familial comfort, mutual celebration of shared power, or the possibility of conspiracy and intelligence gathering. Our heroine is most likely to think:

> I *must* trust others.

Which can also lead to one of my favorite sentiments for my characters, no matter how dire their situation: At least we are in this together.

If you're writing an epic, for example, a thrilling climax for your hero is something along the lines of standing alone against insurmountable odds and defeating the enemy one on one.

But for a heroine, it's more likely to be standing before an army or a team and leading them against a foe together. Or sitting in the background orchestrating matters.

Both of these are positions of power, and as such they empower readers emotionally, just in different ways.

WHOSE JOURNEY IS THIS?

When a hero intrudes on a Heroine's Journey or vice versa

Some very interesting things happen when a hero – and by that, I mean a character whose path is clearly that of a Hero's Journey – intrudes upon a Heroine's Journey.

Another way of putting this is that the main character and the narrative beats are all Heroine's Journey, but into that comes a character who acts and functions autonomously and has the objectives and value system of a hero.

There are two warring elements for writers to keep in mind when a Hero's Journey overlaps into a Heroine's Journey.

1. If you are aware of the intrusion, it can be used to cause conflict on the page that makes for a great story.
2. If you are unaware of it, it can create a potentially

damaging social message via the hero character
and his associated stereotypes.

A hero may make his appearance in a Heroine's Journey as
a side character, a foil, a companion, a lover, or as one of
many in a multiple POV character narrative. Even when
the overarching journey is a Heroine's Journey in terms of
narrative beats, collective goal, and character interaction,
the individuals participating in the story can run the
gamut. In fact, for we writers, there's some serious meat
to be had from these interactions, and fun conflicts to
explore as a result.

For the sake of argument, we can look at the hero inside a
journey not his own, or a heroine inside a journey not her
own, more as archetypes than as representatives of an
alternative journey.

The heroine in the context of a Hero's Journey represents
the feminine (whether biologically female or not).
Because her focus is on cohesion and networking, one can
see how the hero might perceive her as he does most
representatives of femininity – as an instrument of civilization, culture, and stagnation. She wants to keep him,
stop him, divert him to her own path of unity and solidarity, which is the antithesis of his need to be alone and in
motion in order to succeed on his quest.

However, I'd really like to take a look at what happens
when a hero intrudes upon a Heroine's Journey, so let us
start there.

THE HERO INSIDE A HEROINE'S JOURNEY

When the hero appears in a Heroine's Journey, he usually does so as an alpha romantic love interest; while he can be male or female or gender fluid as a character, his presence in the text is gendered masculine.

There are many reasons he is such a popular archetype as a love interest in romance novels. These alpha heroes are very appealing to readers, with their white knight complexes and their hyper-masculine tendencies. They tend to be muscled protectors with violent professions (like soldiers or cops or werewolves), or powerful kingly types with vast wealth and authority (like lonely, emotionally reserved billionaires, rock stars, vampires, and sports celebrities).

These characters are on their own Hero's Journeys and that is the path they intend to tread at the beginning of the book.

Unfortunately for them, if the story they occupy is a Heroine's Journey, they are bound to be saved from their very definition of heroism (solitary action) by the love or friendship of a heroine. I find the intrinsic dichotomy of this push and pull ironically amusing. I used it in my first book, *Soulless,* where the hero, Lord Maccon, really wants to be on a Hero's Journey but my heroine, Alexia, is determined to carry him along with her (and so is his pack). The poor chap doesn't stand a chance.

No isolation for you!

So, the alpha hero starts out lumbering along on his obligatory path of solitude and vengeance, justice and conquering, withdrawal and retrieval of the boon. He intends to be solitary, he is usually written as emotionally reserved (he is a hero; he doesn't want to connect, that would hold him back) and physically powerful (he needs to fight and to win). The hero doesn't trust other characters. He does not try to network, because he absolutely sees himself as deserving of being (and better off) alone.

Inside the Heroine's Journey framework, this character can spiral out of a writer's control. The hero may be depicted positively and yet be verbally or physically abusive, overly possessive (because he sees the heroine as his boon, his earned prize, his reward, and therefore an object) or swerve into stalker territory as his desire for the heroine or what she represents becomes so overwhelming that his own lack of civilization takes over, turning him brutish.

The alpha hero is easily warped when taken in the *context* of a Heroine's Journey – his definition of success is diametrically opposed to hers and thus he can swing too far in the wrong direction. The heroine can *become* his quest – ownership of her will become his definition of victory, which turns him obsessive.

He is already defined by his single-minded pursuit of a goal. When she becomes that goal, he will do anything to have her and to keep her from connecting with anyone but him. He may go so far as to threaten/commit suicide if they are parted or she will not see him. That, of course, instantly comes into conflict with her nature, because what he is doing is isolating her from others and attempting to become her solo network. A heroine doesn't work that way – she wants and needs to build a whole community.

An alpha hero in pursuit of a heroine, when that hero is written closely to the bones of the Hero's Journey, is simultaneously attractive to her as a prospective powerful ally and lover, and dangerous to her in that his objectives are, by their very nature, contrary to hers. This kind of conflict can be very fun to write, but I hope you can also see that it can send an alpha love interest into extremely dangerous territory – readers are prone to calling those kinds of heroes *alpha-holes*.

As you can see, there are minefields and difficulties for storytellers when penning a conflict of archetypes. The precise thing that makes the idea that the heroine might be strong enough in her connective abilities to divert a hero to her path, that she might save him with love, is the exact thing that stands against his nature.

He is designed to resist what she represents, which he will see as seduction, manipulation, and stasis. She represents to him an inability to complete his own journey, so he must sacrifice the very definition of what it means to be a hero (his identity) for her insistence on compromise and family networking. And he doesn't have such a disguise as part of his narrative, unless he's a trickster like Odysseus, but that's a different archetype.

In romance, this idea that the heroine can save her alpha hero with love can work, and work well. In tragic romance, it this element that splits our lovers apart for all eternity.

For writers, the same thing that makes for a good alpha hero makes for the perfect alpha villain.

Who, after all, is more threatening to a heroine than the hero who is compelled to stick to his own journey, a journey where her femininity is to be avoided at all costs? This is rich meat for threat and conflict, as well as love, no matter what your genre. I'll be discussing this further in **Chapter 10** in the section on villains.

THE HEROINE INSIDE A HERO'S JOURNEY

Since the heroine's goals are diametrically opposed to a hero's, she will usually be perceived by the hero in her information-gathering and sharing-of-power modes as manipulative. Her cleverness and skill in doling out power, not to mention her preference for pursuing relationships and stability over victory in battle, will be perceived by the hero in the context of his own narrative as suspicious, if not sinister.

If he sees her positively, he might even be a little afraid of her and the possibility that he might like her too much.

A particularly damaging narrative element that is the result of a heroine intruding upon a Hero's Journey is the archetype of the whore with a heart of gold. A woman who sleeps around, under the umbrella of a Hero's Journey, is the worst example of femininity by his definition.

What she is, of course, is a bastardized version of the ultimate heroine, in that what she is trying to do is establish as many connections as possible, by sleeping with as many people as possible. It's just that she has been warped by being injected into the hero's narrative and perspective on her agency. The act of sleeping around, in this context, implies to our hero that she is not to be trusted – her allegiance may swing to some other hero, perhaps even the villain he will eventually have to face.

THE HERO BECOMING A HEROINE

There is a prevailing theme (in long-running fiction or TV series in particular) of a main character starting out as heroic, but being converted to a heroine through the redemptive lens of the Heroine's Journey. In other words, the journey itself is the agent of change rather than its internal conflict or other characters. I'm thinking particularly of police procedurals and capers.

TV shows with multiple seasons, like *CSI* (2000), or *Leverage* (2008), or even *ER* (1994), are group journeys where characters must work together toward mutual success and common goals, usually the solving of a problem or puzzle. Because the nature of the narrative dictates a need for information gathering and companionship networking, not to mention reliance on outside expert specialists and dependency on each other for safety during the story, the very definition of success in these narratives is good *teamwork*.

The framework for these kinds of procedurals relies on the same themes and messaging that underpins the Heroine's Journey, even though it might not necessarily follow the narrative beats in every episode or season. However, the themes and messages in these dramas do tend to mirror the Heroine's Journey because the definition of success and power is similar.

Interestingly enough, these series inevitably start out with a hero in charge or as a maverick/loner main character. He (and it's usually a gendered masculine character) is the ultimate superior officer, leader, or mastermind who will walk the walk and talk the talk of a hero. He's likely to be hard-bitten, resolved, lonely, separated from his family or in the act of separating, and tends to think of himself as better off on his own (not to mention more successful). Throughout the series, he will constantly try to accomplish things alone, and maintain a belief that he is better and stronger by himself. So, his character evolution is toward becoming a heroine.

His character arc usually ends, in these kinds of series, with his either sacrificing himself for his team (tragic heroine), self-destructing in solitary depression (tragic hero), or successfully completing his shift into heroine and thus embracing marriage (usually to another member of his team) and family and passing along leadership to a subordinate (you go, girl – portion out that power).

Context, therefore, is key when a hero is part of a Heroine's Journey. What was most positive and likely to bring about success for him in a Hero's Journey is now least likely to do so. Either he can adapt his perception of success, of what he thinks is good and what makes him powerful (often the same things), or he cannot.

It's all context driven.

Because of the journey in which he finds himself, a Heroine's Journey, this is literally a case of adapt or die. For readers, he becomes filled with an emotionally powerful pathos under either ending circumstance.

If a hero inside a Heroine's Journey cannot adapt to it, that means he cannot connect with readers of that journey, and they will see him as either profoundly sad or immensely frustrating.

In some cases, because the Heroine's Journey wants him to adapt and become part of its core network, if he doesn't change, readers can feel betrayed.

THE HEROINE BECOMING A HERO

Of course, this also works in the opposite direction. Any heroine inside a Hero's Journey attempting to connect, communicate, network, and unify will be perceived in the context of that journey as weak, slutty, manipulative, or desperate.

Generally speaking, readers of the Hero's Journey will mostly find her frustrating, but it is possible for an adept writer of the Hero's Journey to make her appealing in her very neediness (from the hero's perspective, of course). Incidentally, she also usually dies or sacrifices herself for a heroically noble end (his pursuit of his quest is a good one), because that represents her coming around to the necessity and demands of the Hero's Journey.

However, she can ride off into the sunset all by her lonesome, in pursuit of her own boon, in which case she has successfully made the switch to becoming a hero.

In other words, the narrative is telling us that since the heroine couldn't change the journey itself into a Heroine's Journey, or divert the hero's path into one of her making, the Hero's Journey has won. And readers who enjoy this journey will enjoy that outcome – victory.

When the hero wins, he demands a boon or sacrifice to define his achievement as worthwhile. In other words, if she can't fit the journey, she must die within its pages either in actuality, or the heroine part of her dies, and consumers of the Hero's Journey will love her for it (e.g., Black Widow in the *Avengers* movie franchise).

BUDDIES & SIDEKICKS

We're better together

It is also possible to write a compromise featuring both journeys. Dual narratives or multiple POVs can contain both a hero and a heroine as main characters. Most buddy cop stories (drama or comedy) are a pairing of a hero and a heroine and the two can exist together within the framework of either the Heroine's (comedy) or Hero's (drama) Journey.

Incidentally, I define a buddy narrative as containing what amounts to two main characters having roughly equal page or screen time. As opposed to a sidekick narrative, where there is a main character with a featured support character – see the second section.

BUDDIES

A buddy *comedy*, for example, *Men in Black* (1997), usually features a hard-bitten, sarcastic hero (like Agent K) and a new, enthusiastic heroine (like Agent J). Since it's a comedy, it should come as no surprise that *Men in Black* is a Heroine's Journey, where Agent K sacrifices himself to defeat the bug at the end, as any hero would, but is redeemed by losing his memory and going back to the woman he loves (relations, connection) because he is after all a hero in a Heroine's Journey. While Agent J, our heroine, compromises for position with a new partner (new buddy) and continues to perpetuate a civilizing force.

A buddy *drama*, on the other hand, will usually be a Hero's Journey, and under this framework, the family man side of the equation (our heroine) is going to die and leave the hard-bitten hero buddy to fight on alone.

Under dual narratives circumstances, it is the final scenes and the definition of success that define the framework of the narrative.

If you're writing this kind of story, success is going to be key:

- If success is defined by accomplishing an action together, by good humor and happiness, by ending up as a group or in an organized operation, by finding family or reuniting with old loves, then the chassis is the Heroine's Journey.
- If success is defined by a struggle for rulership or power, a battle for dominance, and a redefining of superiority, then it is a Hero's Journey.

SIDEKICKS

Instead of two main characters, sometimes the weight of dialogue page time and narration (and even POV) is shared with a sidekick. This is a character who accompanies the main character, but the story is clearly not about them. They exist as an assist to the main character (foils can often be sidekicks).

Holmes and Watson are iconic examples of a sidekick narrative. Holmes is, without question, the main character and a hero (self-destructive and solitary), while Watson is more of a heroine. He is a healer, which means communicator and networker, who has injected himself into Holmes's heroic narrative. This works very well for Doyle, and all the various adaptations (I'm looking at you, *House M.D.* 2004).

But those of us who feel deeply about the Heroine's Journey, and perennially yearn for it, ache to see Watson so neglected and even mentally and emotionally abused by Holmes, because we identify so strongly with him and find Holmes, in his single-minded, cruel, solitary braininess, unsympathetic and frustrating.

That is the danger in a sidekick – that the sidekick, being the opposite of the main character, appears put upon or more appealing to readers by contrast.

ARE THESE HEROINE'S OR HERO'S JOURNEYS?

Well, a hero can and often does have a sidekick (sometimes also his foil), who will assist him on his heroic journey and narrative. But usually, since our hero is defined by solitary action, at the very end he will have to defeat his enemy alone. Superhero origin stories, therefore, are often Hero's Journeys, while superhero team stories are often Heroine's Journeys.

An interesting exception to this is *Captain Marvel* (2019), which was (much to my delight and surprise) a buddy cop comedy origin story operating on a Heroine's Journey chassis. The ending sequence is particularly fascinating as she leads a whole group of aliens to their new home (very heroine) and yet she is out in front of them, alone (very hero). Meanwhile, her sidekick gets his reward from a cat alien.

Oh, the symbolism!

Speaking of flerken, this character is the perfect example of a *familiar*, which acts the part of sidekick combined with supernatural assistance or weaponry.

I'm inclined to make the case that certain superheroes are better than others at the different journeys.

Batman, for example, is particularly successful as a hero, because he's very appealing when he engages in a classic Hero's Journey – a grumpy, isolated, withdrawn billionaire whose girlfriends keep dying on him, who wins through physical prowess and usually faces down and defeats one outlandish villain after another. With the exception of the delightfully campy comedy *Batman* TV series (1966–1968), he ultimately fails whenever anyone attempts to write him into a Heroine's Journey or as part of a team – he's too much a hero in the traditional definition of the word.

Spider-Man, on the other hand, nesting comfortably in the realm of YA, and coming-of-age or *bildungsroman* narratives, can successfully undertake either journey, depending on which growth pattern you want to see him ultimately evolve into (hero or heroine).

But back to the sidekick discussion.

Heroines almost *have* to have a sidekick, or buddy, or best friend, or multiple versions thereof. Since heroines are the doyennes of information gathering, they must network or fail.

> Any narrative involving a heroine will also involve her companions.

Sidekicks can and do range around species as well. Animal sidekicks/familiars are common (I'm looking at you, Disney). From a writer's perspective, these are perennially popular and add excellent color to your narrative, but they are practically demanded by the Heroine's Journey within certain genres. Cozy mysteries and urban fantasies in particular are prone to featuring esoteric animal friends. Cats often act like tiny, complaining hero sidekicks or tricksters, while dogs and horses are usually depicted with more heroine attitudes.

Incidentally, children can also fill the role of sidekick.

A sidekick is usually partly or wholly dependent on the main character for survival (or in the case of cop dramas, promotion). For a heroine in particular, a child or animal sidekick is so dependent upon her that they become an incredibly secure and vital network point, and she will (and should, if you want readers to like her) do anything in her power to maintain that connection and protect her sidekick from peril.

Which brings us to comedy and genres like cozy mysteries, in which the sidekick will almost always provide a *last-minute assist* either with physical prowess or information, or by getting kidnapped in order to drive the main character into rescue operations.

Why?

Because, once again, these stories are most likely to exist inside a Heroine's Journey framework.

FOILS & DUALITIES

Getting literary for a moment

If you're familiar with critical analysis of the *Iliad*, for example, you'll be aware of the concept of literary foils.

A foil is basically a character who defines another character by contrast. Patroclus is essentially the feminine foil (and conscience) for Achilles. He might even be thought of as the Heroine's Journey attempt to save Achilles from his tragic yet inevitable Hero's Journey path.

For those of us in the fantasy arena, Frodo and Sam in *The Lord of the Rings* are interesting to consider. Is Sam merely Frodo's sidekick, or is Sam actually Frodo's foil? Tolkien may be having a conversation with us in which Frodo represents the officer class, and Sam the long-suffering enlisted soldiers from World War I. Picture Sam carrying Frodo at the end, literally lifting up the officer class, corrupted by the power they must both try to destroy.

Foil relationships don't always fit cleanly into one journey or another.

Part of that is because the foil character often represents the feminine being dragged into the Hero's Journey, where her objective (networking) is diametrically opposed to the main character's need for victory at all costs, so that the cost will usually be to the foil.

Alternatively, the heroine's foil will represent the masculine and carry the objectives of the Hero's Journey inside a Heroine's Journey, in which case he's probably obsessed with winning and keeps trying to go off on his own to kill things.

In *The Lord of the Rings*, the climatic final sequences where the objective is ultimate ring destruction, Frodo literally cannot let go of the ring and the power it represents (hero), while Sam ends up carrying Frodo and the ring together in a glaring example of support network in action (heroine).

Sam the foil (representing both heroine and common man) will *never* leave his friend behind; he is defined by this trait. Sam also earns a classic Heroine's Journey ending – home, hearth, and family. Sam loses Frodo, which is against his nature, but we leave him settled full circle within the embrace of his hobbit community.

Frodo, of course, has the classic bittersweet Greek hero's end. Broken down by his quest and no longer fit to occupy the very world he managed to save, Frodo must move on to the next.

In the end, both characters have engaged in successful versions of their respective journeys.

DUELING JOURNEYS

Which leads us to buddy cop dramas and comedies. Movies like *Men in Black* (1997) and *Captain Marvel* (2019), or the original *Star Trek* TV series (1966) often showcase foils through conflicting examples of heroes, heroines, or both. In some cases, those foils become something more like sidekicks, or even develop into two or more main characters.

Writing a dual dynamic can be great fun. By dual dynamic, I mean a story written from two opposed POV characters: one from a hero's perspective and the other from a heroine's, or from the perspective of two heroes with different objectives, or two heroines with different networks.

It's a writerly challenge to balance quest and purpose against conflicting ultimate goals of two different heroes (many buddy cop dramas), or two different heroines (many dual spy or heist comedies), or more commonly one of each heroic type. Often the two protagonists will inhabit one journey in an uneasy balance. I'll be talking about how to approach crossing journeys in the next section.

6

MULTIPLE POV NARRATIVES

So many voices in my head

In genre fiction especially, there's the added complexity of writing multiple POV narratives.

Examples of this kind of ensemble cast include space operas like *Firefly* (2002), epic fantasies like *Game of Thrones* (2011), or sweeping historical fiction and generational family sagas. These kinds of narratives can feature multiple versions of heroes, heroines, foils, sidekicks, and buddies, all in the same narrative.

There are so many different characters on so many different versions of various journeys that these multiple POV works can become too complicated to comfortably inhabit either journey. Often, it's even difficult to tell what journey any individual character is on until the very end.

In genre fiction, multiple point of view narratives are generally the province of epic fantasy, like *Game of Thrones* (2011), political upheaval melodramas, family sagas, and space operas. Soap operas, medical shows, and procedurals like *Law & Order* (1990) or *CSI* (2000) also fall into this category. Sweeping political space operas like *The Expanse* (2015) or *Battlestar Galactica* (2004) also defy being pigeonholed into either narrative.

All of these can (and usually do) feature multiple heroes, and sometimes a few heroines as well, working toward a collective goal, or against each other in flexibly misaligned groups.

HEROES AND HEROINES IN GROUPS

Generally speaking, a hero does not do teamwork well. That, of course, then becomes one of the writer's narrative tools for conflict, playing on the fact that all your heroes lack the capacity to be anything but solitary victors.

Let the back-stabbing drama commence!

Remember, for the hero, groups are dangerous, so when he is in a narrative situation where he must play nice within a group, that alone becomes a tremendous vehicle for conflict.

On the flip side, heroines in multiple POV narratives are going to work hard to build or rebuild something *together*. Capers or heist narratives, political fantasies involving positive representations of diplomacy, military rescue missions, or something like a planetfall science fiction with a foundational survivor narrative all work well using the Heroine's Journey as the chassis for multiple POVs.

Anything where a group is thrown together and *must* work together for a common good (and you, as the author, intend a positive outcome with no tragedy allowed) is going to fit comfortably into the Heroine's Journey.

Under these circumstances, dramas where the conflict comes from an outside source, such as natural disaster, alien invasion, or a super challenging physical environments/games, will likely work best for heroines. Your human enemies coming from within the group are most likely to have a hero's mentality of solo action and violent tendencies.

Your heroines, when a group is under threat by any party, are likely to respond by turning into generals – delegating responsibility and recognizing who is best at what task.

Conflict can also arise when a heroine's judgements or directional choices are questioned. When multiple heroines are in play, they may each identify different approaches to networking and success, and this can be a great way to write multiple likable characters who all seem reasonable to the readers but ultimately have different solutions that put them into conflict with each other.

When there are multiple heroes and heroines in one group:

Heroes are more likely to have different or conflicting *goals*.

Heroines are more likely to have different or conflicting *approaches* to the same goal.

CHAPTER 9: READER EXPERIENCE

Writing to please yourself and your readers

I have already mentioned the concept of reader betrayal. In this part, we are going to explore it in more depth, as well as the notion of reader expectations (flip sides of the same coin). You see, these tie not only to narrative beats, tropes, and archetypes, but also to the emotional experience readers have as part of the journey they unconsciously expect.

In other words, we are going to look at what readers inadvertently tell us they want when they review a book or TV show or movie, positively or negatively. Yes, we writers can control these things. Yes, it is absolutely our responsibility to do so. And yes, it is tied to the Heroine's Journey.

I was on a panel recently where someone asked one of those questions I dread, all about the sacred nature of art. Essentially:

"Shouldn't we be writing to please ourselves?"

To which my answer is:

"Sure, but then you know the size of your audience, right? One. You."

If you want to write to please yourself, keep a diary. If you want to write and have other people read it, then you're going to have to think about actually providing a satisfying experience to an audience that exists out there in the world.

Honestly?

Selfishness is always boring. And you can cause irreparable damage with unconscious exclusion.

There's an insidious underpinning to this kind of question at play as well. The cry of "Art for art's sake," and "I'm only doing this to please myself; I don't have to take the opinions of others into account," is a cry that has been used for a very long time, mostly by the powerful elite as a reason why they (who have the largest platform and biggest audience) do not need to take minority voices into account. It has given us the same type of writer – old, white, straight, and male – writing the same type of story for generations.

A variety of stories need to be told and valued, including those that rely on a Heroine's Journey and those which highlight new voices that appeal to a wide range of readers.

I believe that fiction writers not only *must* consider their audience for commercial reasons, but that we also have a duty, as the purveyors of modern cultural narratives, to do so.

I write commercial genre fiction and that is what interests me. Which means I need and want to take my readers and what they desire into account or I won't sell any books. But I also want my books to have an emotional impact on my audience. In my case, I want to perpetuate warmth and hope.

I can best reach my readers through the Heroine's Journey, and they have inadvertently told me that this works for them over and over again by buying my books in sufficient quantities to give me a living. (Which I'm hoping is the ultimate goal for any professional storyteller.) Consequently, I've realized more and more that the Heroine's Journey is what they're hungry for because its guiding principle is *connection*, and that leads to comfort.

In addition to a greater understanding of reader desire, not to mention the world around us and pop culture, knowing the Heroine's Journey can have three profound *concrete* effects on the *craft* of writing:

1. It can help us better manage reader expectations.

2. It can help us with writer's block mid-story.
3. It can help prevent reader betrayal.

I'm going to go through all three of these concrete effects, and hopefully help writers avoid any pitfalls connected with them.

READER EXPECTATIONS

Narrative has the power

If you know the good and the bad of both journeys, and which one you're writing, then you have the power to manage your reader and audience expectations.

As writers of fiction, our primary function is to tell an entertaining story well, but our secondary goal should be to manage reader expectations in every possible way. For the sake of ease, I'm going to use the moniker *reader*, but for you screenwriters or audiophiles out there, please know I also mean *watcher, viewer,* and *listener*.

MANAGING READER EXPECTATIONS

So, what do I mean by *managing reader expectations*?

Well, basically, this is how a storyteller keeps interest and enhances the immersion experience for their audience. Yes, plot and pace play key roles, but they are not the only tools we have access to.

How many of you have sat through a thrilling action movie and yet never felt drawn into the characters or drama? That weird, niggling sense of *I know I was supposed to enjoy it, but I just didn't, and I don't really know why.*

The heartbeat of narrative (whether Heroine's or Hero's Journey) is the chassis upon which your story runs (whether intentionally or not) and provides readers with a culturally endemic subconscious foreshadowing.

You can absolutely play with and manipulate your readers by simulating one journey, only to twist it into another – so long as you realize this is one of the most frustrating things you can do to an audience.

In other words, if you are telling a Heroine's Journey, readers have certain expectations of that journey, quite apart from all the genre or subgenre expectations. For example, the expectations of a romance novel include a happy ending. Your cover and blurb might showcase other tropes and archetypes that carry their own sets of expectations for your subgenre of romance, e.g., a vampire love interest for paranormal or a billionaire hero for contemporary.

But as you're writing a Heroine's Journey (which you are if you write romance), there are other unconscious themes you are also setting up that a reader may not be able to explicitly name but which they yearn for *because of the underpinning Heroine's Journey*. If these are neglected, underdeveloped, or absent, a reader will feel the lack and perhaps write a bad review, or worse, lose faith in you as a storyteller and ignore your work henceforth.

If present, a subtle use of the Heroine's Journey will enhance the experience: employing themes of connection, family, and cohesion as well as that happy ending; themes of asking for and receiving help; of sibling affection (or betrayal) and so forth – all, in fact, of the markers of a heroine's Descent, Search, and Ascent that I have been harping on, lo, these last many pages.

This is not the beat or even the melody of the song you are singing, it is something more profound, more basic. It is the notion of the music itself, and how rhythm and voice conjoin to give an immersive experience to others. Without this underpinning, your story can die during its creation because it doesn't resonate with you, the creator, or it will not gain traction with readers.

When expectations are not met, a reader will feel unsatisfied with the ending, and in retrospect, the entire story. They may become angry with the book and often, also, the author. Repercussions are severe not just for reviews, popularity, and sales of that book, but for other books from the same author in the future.

You see, the writer has broken their reader's trust in their storytelling ability. Readers find that very difficult to forgive.

EMOTIONAL HOOKS & WRITER'S BLOCK

What readers are looking for emotionally and how this can help writers to keep writing

So what emotional resonance are readers of the different journeys looking for? How do we as story tellers give them what they truly desire?

WHAT DO READERS OF THE HERO'S JOURNEY WANT?

Hero's Journey books are described positively by readers in reviews and blogs as

- Thrilling
- Dramatic
- Rough
- Tough
- Violent
- Hard boiled
- Raunchy
- Wicked
- Heart palpitating
- Fast paced
- Edgy

From these emotion-laden words (I sometimes call them *hooks*) and the general tenor of the reader base, I feel it's safe to conclude that what readers of the Hero's Journey are primarily looking for is...

EXCITEMENT

Examples of authors who write such books include Ian Fleming, Raymond Chandler, and the modern scions of this style like Lee Child. In fantasy and science fiction, they run the gamut from Frank Herbert and Robert Heinlein to Brent Weeks and Andy Weir.

WHAT DO READERS OF THE HEROINE'S JOURNEY WANT?

Heroine's Journey books are described positively by readers in reviews and blogs as

- Sexy
- Sweet
- Warm or heartwarming
- Charming
- Funny
- Witty
- Calm
- Quiet
- Delightful
- Addictive
- Romantic
- Sentimental

From these words and the general tenor of readers describing what they love and search for (including yours truly), I feel it's safe to conclude that what readers want from the Heroine's Journey is…

COMFORT

Comfort in the story itself, looking for the author to provide on-page friendships, likable characters, and happy endings, and also finding comfort in the predictability of the story's underlying pattern, in the service of which the author must satisfy (or at least nod to) certain tropes, archetypes, theses, and positive messages.

In other words, we want comfort to be represented both in *what* we write, and in *how* we write it.

Examples of authors who write such books include Jane Austen, Georgette Heyer, Beverly Jenkins, and the reigning queen of romance, Nora Roberts. In fantasy and science fiction, you'll find Mercedes Lackey, Anne McCaffrey, Lois McMaster Bujold, and Naomi Novik.

HOW THIS HELPS WITH WRITER'S BLOCK

As storytellers, knowing which narrative journey our POV character is on, and the pitfalls of each, can profoundly help us not only to manage reader expectations, but also to construct for ourselves a fantastic toolbox of elements that help us avoid writer's block.

If you're writing a Hero's Journey and you're up against a wall?

Your hero probably needs to make a decision that gets him into motion and isolated. That is the only way he is going to accomplish something narratively meaningful. He needs a goal, a quest, and he needs a powerful ability that defines him as the only one able to accomplish this task.

Or you can throw a temptation at him – a seductress, or a dangerous situation. Put him in a crowd with a bomb about to go off. Have his enemy try to trap him (AKA keep him still).

Or you can go back to the words of emotion at the beginning of this section, and revisit what readers hunt for in this journey: excitement.

The same kinds of tricks hold true for working our way out of a plot pickle when writing the Heroine's Journey.

Got your heroine stuck somewhere?

Introduce a helpful new character, make a new friend, throw on a disguise, have the main character start portioning out tasks to friends, have your character consult an expert, give her a new familiar or sidekick (or kink, heh heh), introduce a hero to help or to hinder her journey, since his objectives will naturally cause tension with hers.

Just take a look at where you are in her journey (Descent, Search, Ascent?) and go back to the basics. Look at the myths – they will guide you and offer (to my mind) seemingly endless options.

Divide your love interest into fourteen parts and scatter him over the Nile Valley... metaphorically speaking, of course. A fake phallus, new baby, and resurrection of a dead body works wonders for any plot, if you ask me. Not to mention a hungry fish.

Revisit your audience's emotional expectations

Returning to the emotional words used in positive reviews can help you as a writer, both to overcome your own hiccups and to guide what you might choose to write next. Use these words to determine how you can pitch your work after it is complete, how you describe it in blurbs or to editors and agents, and how you might sell it or market it.

Already written a few books?

You can visit your own positive reader reviews, if you have more than one book out, and see what terms readers apply to your work. Or take a look at top sellers in your subgenre to tease out the specifics of the market right now.

My own books are often described as *charming* and *witty*, so charming wit is what I try to give back to my readers, every single time, regardless of genre.

And comfort, always comfort.

A helpful and relatively brief spate of research you can do is to pick the top ten books in the subgenre you're interested in writing, going as narrow as possible for that subgenre – contemporary gay romantic suspense, historical buddy cop, cozy mystery, whatever it may be – and read a few of the five-star reviews of those books. Fortunately for us, reviews from nonprofessionals will mostly focus on parroting back the plot (not important for this investigation) and then *their emotional response* (absolutely fascinating).

It's this second part that is particularly useful.

- What words do they use?
- Would those apply to your own work?
- Be honest with yourself, because this is an opportunity to learn and possibly revise.

Incidentally, yeah, it's perfectly valid to use these emotion words in your marketing copy after you've gone to the bother of figuring them out and deciding whether they apply to your book. I've always loved the old trick for writing essays:

> Tell them what you're gonna say, say it, then tell them what you said.

As I said early on, this also works great for sex and dirty talk in fiction. Have your characters tell each other what they wanna do, do it, and then talk about what they did. This allows you, the storyteller, to wrap consent, action, and hotness, all in one lovely package. Yummy.

But I digress.

I find that this technique of gathering up the emotionally positive words from readers works great in book blurbs, pitching, and advertising. Let's face it, it's hard for most writers to promote themselves. You see, whichever journey you're writing is doing this heavy lifting for you – it can point you in the direction not only of narrative beats, but also toward emotional responses.

> And really, if you write, isn't that what you want to engender in your readers – an emotional response?

So, after you've taken a look to see what emotion words and adjectives reviewers use to describe the most popular books in your genre, you not only know better what you're writing, but in some cases you can also use these to guide pivot points in your book (both plot and pace), including your main character's actions, behavior, and choices.

Bye-bye writer's block.

These words can also help you determine, for example, that perhaps the story you're writing is not going to fit well in the genre where you think it belongs. If the words you keep running into actually do *not* describe your book in any way, you're focusing on the wrong genre or subgenre, or even the wrong heroic journey altogether.

Genres and subgenres, as I've already discussed, may be dominated by one journey over another. Or your book may be one of those that rides happily on a melding of the two, like dual narratives, and you simply need to apply the emotive attributes and adjectives to one or the other character in your multicharacter piece to appeal to the ideal audience.

3

AVOIDING READER BETRAYAL

Or, how to stop readers from throwing your book at a wall

I go to various cafés in my city, as one does when one is an author. I like to try out new ones, see if they have something I particularly like to drink or eat. One day, I discovered a new one that had good ambiance and nice beverages, but I wasn't sure about the food.

I was hungry, so I decided to order a sandwich.

A grave mistake.

You see, they had a *Reuben* listed on the menu. This is one of my favorite sandwiches and traditionally it is made with five basic things:

1. Corned beef
2. Swiss cheese
3. Sauerkraut
4. Russian dressing
5. Rye bread

Here is what I was served:

1. Pastrami
2. American cheese
3. Caramelized onions
4. Mayo
5. Sourdough bread

I will admit that sometimes the meat of a Reuben is pastrami and not corned beef. I will even admit that sometimes it's Thousand Island dressing instead of Russian. But what I was served had only one (tentative) crossover element, the pastrami. This was no Reuben, it was a pastrami melt.

When the sandwich was brought to me, I could see without tasting that it was not on rye bread. I immediately questioned whether they had brought the correct sandwich. They told me that at this café, the Reuben came on sourdough.

Ooookaaaay?

Then, when I bit into it and there was no tang, only creaminess, I stood up and took it back to the counter. I was honestly confused. I had a whole conversation about what was going on. Were they sure I'd got the right sandwich? Yes. But where was the kraut? The Swiss cheese? *Anything that made this an actual Reuben?*

I was informed that this was how *they made their Reubens.*

I finished my drink, did not eat my sandwich, and left feeling forlorn and sad and disappointed by life. I have never returned to that café.

And that, everyone, is the gastro equivalent of reader betrayal.

I was led to believe that what I was about to consume was one thing. I was even convinced to keep trying it *despite* the packaging. It turned out to be *nothing* like I expected.

Nothing.

Reader betrayal can take many forms. At its root, it is the sensation a reader gets when the book they're reading does something totally unexpected in a *bad* way. For example, when a book they picked up thinking it was romance doesn't have a happy ending. Sometimes it's the fault of the cover or the blurb (or the trailer or the posters in the case of movies and TV) and sometimes it's a flaw in story structure. Those first few things we writers don't always have control over.

But the story, well, that is a writer's domain. And also a writer's responsibility.

We make promises to our readers in our blurbs on the backs of our books, in the title, and in the first few parts. These are the first bites the reader takes of our writing, and they will know from the flavor and taste whether they want to continue, whether the book is for them. Occasionally they will put it down and walk away, because it's not for them. It's just not their kind of sandwich, so to speak.

But worse, far worse, is when readers think they are on one journey, or are reading one genre, and everything we wrote led them into that expectation... and then it turns out it wasn't that kind of book at all. That's not just a shrug and a moment of disappointment, that's true reader betrayal.

If you're lucky, they leave you a one-star review. If you're unlucky, they slag you off to all their friends and never read anything you write ever again.

READER BETRAYAL FROM A STORY PERSPECTIVE

You know that time when you're reading a book and you're perfectly happy with it, or watching a TV series, and then suddenly something shifts in the plot, and you want to hurl heavy objects?

That's reader betrayal.

Why does reader betrayal happen?

- Often a flaw in story structure: You're reading one thing, when the writer suddenly takes a dive and turns it into something else. That is the writer's fault. (This is what I call the *scream and hurl* scenario.)
- Or it can be a flaw in the reader's expectations. She thought she was reading one kind of book, despite the cover and blurb trying to tell her otherwise, and she read it anyway. That's something we writers *can't* control.

One of the best ways to avoid reader betrayal?

Know your narrative journey, know which one you're writing or exactly how you're combining them, and know the expectations of the genre or subgenre in which you nest.

A post-apocalyptic YA Hero's Journey (*Divergent*, 2011) is going to look a lot different from a post-apocalyptic YA

Heroine's Journey (*The Hunger Games*, 2008). Both will have to hit the archetypes and tropes of a post-apocalyptic coming-of-age reader's desires, but they will have different narrative elements based on the journey as well.

At its soul, the biggest form of reader betrayal when adhering to a Heroine's Journey narrative is a pivot in plot that suddenly emphasizes success in isolation, or a pivot in character so that the heroine suddenly becomes a vengeful, violent solitary hero.

Readers of the Heroine's Journey are hunting for sensations of found family and support. They are hungry for connection and unity, friendship and love (platonic or otherwise). If they feel that your main character or even your author voice doesn't believe in this anymore, or your narrative takes them in a direction that emphasizes the opposite of what is morally *good*, they will be angry with you, the storyteller.

They may not be able to articulate that this is going on, but they will be mad about it.

The *Battlestar Galactica* reboot (2004) is a particularly interesting case study. For all intents and purposes, it started out as a Heroine's Journey. After all, what is Laura's forever cry but *finding home, staying alive, and staying together*. There is literally a board with the population number on it, a physical representation of increasing connection. During its first few seasons, *Battlestar Galactica* (2004) explores themes of unity, cohesion, and staying together. Then it twists to become a Hero's Journey full of glorification of the individual in battle, ideas of prophecy, privacy, betrayal, and solo excellence. I'd argue this is one of the reasons behind the prevailing sensation of fan betrayal that colored the final season of this show. We were led into the assumption of one narrative, it became another, forgot where it was and what it was doing, and fizzled out.

By knowing and following the chassis of the Heroine's Journey, writers can manage readers' expectations and prevent the sensation of betrayal. Add the application of tropes and archetypes essential to your specific subgenre and you can give readers what they truly want from a commercial fiction story – the heartbeat of familiarity combined with your unique voice and approach to the overarching style. Readers will stick with you and come back again and again for more, because they will associate you with this kind of reassurance and innate sense of satisfaction.

You'll become a favorite restaurant, so to speak.

What I am saying is, build the best Reuben, put your unique twist on it of course, change one or two elements if you must. But if you tell them it's a Reuben, ensure that the sandwich is, in fact, a Reuben.

Then, if they like your take on it, they will come back again and again. They might even try a different sandwich, because if you did it for them once, they'll be fairly confident you can do it again.

If they don't like your take on a Reuben, they aren't your reader.

But if you promise a Reuben and what you deliver is a pastrami melt?

They will leave and never return.

You are best served by making your promises to your readers based on which journey you are using, as well as which genre you inhabit. Only then will you leave your audience satisfied and you can begin building an author brand that rests on readers trusting your voice.

CHAPTER 10: HOW TO WRITE LIKE A HEROINE

Beating the drum

In this section we are going to delve into what *exactly* you can write to ensure you're not only hitting the Heroine's Journey narrative beats, but providing for reader satisfaction as well, and cultivating their eventual inevitable obsession with your work.

I'm going to lay out all my secrets. The practical things you can do to make sure you're writing the kind of Heroine's Journey that is long lived and beloved and obsessed over by readers and fans and even, occasionally, fellow writers.

First, one last time, with feeling, the beats of the journey are:

HEROINE'S JOURNEY BEATS

The Descent

Broken familial network.

Pleas ignored and abdication of power.

Involuntary withdrawal.

Offers of aid but no solution.

The Search

Loss means isolation/risk.

Disguise/subversion.

Formation of surrogate network.

Visit to the underworld, aided by companions.

The Ascent

Success means new/reborn familial network.

She excels at delegating, networking, communicating, and portioning out tasks and achievement.

Her negotiation and compromise benefits all.

Revenge and glory are not important.

Remember, these beats do not have to be your outline – they are guides to how you might construct a chassis of narrative. You don't have to hit every single one.

These are pointers toward plot, not necessarily the plot itself. They do not have to be in the exact order presented (see Inanna) or weighted equally. They can be repeated.

Elements can appear out of order (or not at all) and your story will still be a Heroine's Journey so long as the touch-stones remain consistent.

So long as your main character's success is vested in networking; so long as her strength is in asking for help; so long as all the things you love about a Heroine's Journey are present in your book, that book will find an audience that loves those same elements and wants to give them back to you, the author.

Okay, so how exactly do we activate it?

Let me count the ways. There are ten.

GIVE YOUR HEROINE COMPANIONS

For storytellers, perhaps the most important signal marker of a Heroine's Journey is ensuring that you give your main character plenty of friends. True friends, lovable and loving companions. Complex friends with depth to them, who may occasionally be led astray, but who always return (sometimes instantly, sometimes not until the very end of the story), who offer and try to help to the best of their abilities.

Simply put, they act to strengthen the heroine *as a heroine* with their presence.

You can also populate your universe not only with friends, but also with acquaintances, familiars, sidekicks, animal companions, helpers, aids, teachers, and more.

MULTIPLE LIKABLE CHARACTERS

If you're writing a Heroine's Journey, it's absolutely *vital* to write multiple likable characters.

One of the best examples of this is the Weasley family in the Harry Potter franchise. Ron is, of course, Harry's best friend and sidekick (and often comic relief). As the series progresses, the rest of the Weasley family also becomes vital to Harry's journey. They remain comic relief, but they are also well-rounded and able-bodied companions and helpers whenever needed. Their moments of family happiness (holidays, weddings, ugly sweaters) shift to absorb Harry, furthering their connection to him, with him, and for him.

Readers remember and resonate with moments where members of the Weasley family step forward to protect and help Harry. Mrs Weasley in particular, as the mother figure, has a powerful role to play with readers. Her moments in the final battle – defending Ginny and losing a child – have such a profound impact because she is the ultimate representation of a heroine's familial connection, compassion, protection, and love. A great deal of this has to do with how key Mrs Weasley is to Harry as a member of his support network. You and I know, and so does every reader, that if Harry needed Mrs Weasley, she would move heaven and earth to help him. And yet, she is a very minor character.

As a storyteller, you can build up these complex, lovable side characters further by having them help not only the heroine, but each other too. The Weasleys host the rebellion, for example. (Also, putting them under threat is a powerful stressor on your audience and your heroine's motivation.)

It's important to show that these characters don't only exist for your main character, but that they have their own lives and interests, and that their helpfulness is part of their intrinsic nature, not just something they trot out when your heroine is in need. This gives them more rounded personalities and a wider appeal. Also, it gives readers alternate characters to identify with, so they can see themselves in your books, even if it's only in a minor character.

HEALTHY PLATONIC FRIENDSHIPS

In particular, healthy platonic friendships on the page are a rare and unique gift to readers. By that, I mean nonsexual confidantes providing support to each other.

Friendship between straight men and straight women, gay men and other gay men, gay women and other gay women, and all the nuances of each, are rare in fiction, yet are profoundly important.

These are characters who don't want to sleep with each other, who will *never* sleep with each other, and who can have and hold together a solid relationship without a sexual component. They showcase mental and emotional intimacy, which is often forgotten about in fiction, or shown only as a minor part of sexual intimacy.

Oversexualization of friendship ties back to the archetypes of the Hero's Journey, where the presence of the feminine in a hero's narrative (and with it, sexual seduction) is a threat and is sexualized under almost all circumstances. This gives us a prevailing culture concept that the primary focus of a relationship where sex is a possibility should be sex *first* and the autonomy of the character a distant second. The lens of the POV hero character becomes focused on the sexual gratification they can get from any given relationship.

Contrary to this, the focus of the heroine on any relationship, sexual or not, will be:

> "What are the strengths and weaknesses of my friend and how can we help each other?"

Perpetuating the idea that all intimate relationships carry with them the baggage of sexual attraction is profoundly damaging, and it is also the antithesis of the Heroine's Journey - whether you're writing a romance thread or not.

FRIENDS ARE LOYAL

Similarly, the idea that feminine friends, or best friends, always betray and stab each other in the back for fun and plotting is deeply troubling to denizens of the Heroine's Journey.

Back-stabbing is used as a means to isolate a heroine, but it comes from a hero's perspective, with an idea toward the hero thriving in isolation. It also says something profoundly damaging to the reader about your heroine main character:

> This heroine cannot trust her own judgment in terms of networking.

This concept attacks the very core of a heroine's identity and motivation – communication and networking is her *strength*. In the context of the Heroine's Journey, a betrayal from a friend, especially a feminine friend or sisterhood, diminishes and trivializes the heroine's own identity.

Your readers will feel betrayed by this and experience a similar lack of trust in you as an author and in your main character's judgment going forward. Instead of building sympathy, when a friend backstabs a heroine, readers are likely not only to hate the friend, but to become innately suspicious of your main character too.

So, not just platonic friendships but *loyal* friendships are extremely important to the Heroine's Journey.

SEXUALIZING THE HEROINE

This is not to say that good sex and sexual relationships aren't an option for the heroine.

There's a reason, after all, that romance novels are the Heroine's Journey. This is because sexual union for a heroine is, without question, an opportunity for emotional support and connection and power.

But the point is that it's not her *only* avenue to intimacy. Not even in a romance novel.

In broad brush strokes, when writing the Heroine's Journey our narrative hinges on positive acts of intimacy, information exchange, and friendship between characters as models of power.

> In practical terms, this means that dialogue and love scenes tend to carry more weight and page time in Heroine's Journeys.

Before you ask, yes, there are absolutely ways to write a fight scene that highlights connection and relationships between warriors, between knights in battle, cowboys in a shootout, soldiers at war, and so forth. There is a reason the buddy cop comedy is a *thing*. Who survives the battle and how, and the construction of whether the intimacy in violence is about connection and mutual success, or whether it is about sacrifice so that the hero can win, distinguishes the two narrative types.

A core theme behind the Heroine's Journey is that friendly relationships are an opportunity for growth, for movement forward (emotional, mental, physical), and for success in the journey. That is the heroine's first priority in meeting new people – the possibility of a relationship, not a threat or competition.

***

From an author-business perspective, one of the best things about creating appealing side characters, friends, lovers, and family for your heroine is that readers will fall in love with and cry out for more from even the most minor of helpers. They see them as shining beacons of aid to their beloved main character.

Then you, the author, can stay in your universe and continue to write more, turning one of your side characters into your next heroine. Because that is, of course, what the best side characters *are* in the context of this narrative – they are also all heroines themselves, each one on her own Heroine's Journey. Because the heroine has a mutually beneficial relationship with her companions, those companions do not have to die or sacrifice themselves in order for her narrative to be successful.

> Side characters can live on to become heroines in their own right.

This is such rich meat for writers. As readers and fans grow to love your side characters, those side characters become main characters and go on to have books of their own.

Let's be honest here – I built an entire career on this premise.

DEFINE & JOIN A GROUP

In addition to writing individual side characters with reader appeal, the group dynamic is also key to a successfully executed Heroine's Journey. For our heroine, the group represents an opportunity to connect and gather information to further her journey.

This narrative almost always emphasizes family (found or blood); friendship groups; and shared values, morals, and/or ethics. Therefore, a certain tribalism or notion of belonging to a group within the context of a greater whole should be emphasized.

A fantastic example of this in action is the Hogwarts Houses in the Harry Potter books. A truly genius invention, they not only give the student characters in the series alternate familial groups and shared value systems, but they also give readers encouragement to form allegiances with each other under the purview of explicitly defined identities. Dividing a magical system, or a school, or a world, or a spaceship (yellow, blue, or red shirt?) into groups that emphasize both ability and personality is a codified way of shorthanding found family.

Readers can immediately test into and identify where they might *belong*. And because they are reading a Heroine's Journey partly *for* that sensation of belonging, this is intensely satisfying for an audience. After all, *belonging* is a major source of comfort.

If your story universe delineates clear ways to include not only your heroine and her friends, but also your readers, that's an assured path to intimately involve an audience in a narrative experience.

I've done this, for example, by offering my readers a way to devise their own Parasol Protectorate code name (the most frivolous piece of clothing you own + favorite dessert). Early on in my career, I offered them a quiz to test whether they were werewolf, vampire, ghost, or soulless.

The Heroine's Journey is particularly easy to adapt to this approach, and it can be great fun for you and your audience to come up with informal quizzes or surveys, not to mention discussions in fan groups about where they might belong and why. The Harry Potter books changed a whole generation into defining their own personalities by Hogwarts Houses.

Before you ask about my house:

> I want to be a Hufflepuff, I act like a Gryffindor, I've a career as a Ravenclaw, but I'm probably a Slytherin.

WRITE APPROPRIATE VILLAINS

I've talked about friends and walk-on characters who serve to assist our heroine, but what about those who wish to thwart her?

The best villain for a heroine is one who is bent on separating her from her support network. After all, it is the act of separation that precipitates her descent, the first step on her journey:

- Hades kidnaps Persephone
- Set kills and scatters Osiris
- demons dog Inanna demanding a sacrifice (fine, Inanna kinda brings these things down on herself, but you get my drift)
- Voldemort kills Harry's whole family, for goodness sake. Even the horcruxes damage Harry's friendship support system.

So, when you're writing villains, it's a great idea to have them attempt to separate your POV characters from each other. They can do this physically or mentally or emotionally. The best school bully, for example, is one who manages to turn the heroine's friends against her through peer pressure and conversation.

> Could anything be more evil to a heroine than the activation of her own social network against her?

Voldemort is constantly trying to isolate Harry, to separate him from others. Even Dumbledore's continual (apparent) motivation to isolate Harry and withhold important information might cause us to perceive him as a villain. I often wonder if Dumbledore is there to represent the Hero's Journey mentor, as he keeps trying to put Harry on the path of hero, with himself in the mentor role. (Destined to die, of course, as a result). Under those circumstances his attempts to isolate Harry might be perceived as his trying to force Harry to become a hero (possibly a pathos-driven, self-sacrificing one) when Harry is, in fact, a heroine on a Heroine's Journey and so will defy Dumbledore's intent by never going it alone.

THE HERO INSIDE A HEROINE'S JOURNEY CAN BE A VILLAIN

Some other fun things you can do with bad guys, as a writer of this journey? Disguise your heroes as villains and villains as heroes.

The hero on a Hero's Journey within the context of a Heroine's Journey is a danger to himself and others, and probably a threat to the heroine. His presence in her narrative is complicated and fraught with danger for both characters. He can end up being a good, complicated love interest – if the heroine can redeem him by teaching him the ways of her journey and diverting him to her narrative of love, compassion, compromise, and networking.

He can also be a useful friend.

As Isis sends Horus off on a quest that suits his particular set of skills, so too can your heroine activate her friendly neighborhood hero (likely to be a family member or former lover). I mean, if he is bent on sacrificing himself for the greater good and whacking others with pointy objects, she might as well make use of that inclination, right? If she's really good at her journey, she might even manage to keep him from killing himself or dying alone and lonely.

He can also make for a great tragic love interest.

If he cannot be redeemed or diverted from his path, he will leave her heartbroken in order to pursue his own agenda, riding off into the sunset alone to retrieve his boon and conquer the enemy. This can even be the separation that starts your heroine on her descent.

Alternatively, the true hero also makes a wonderful villain – his course of solitary action and victory through violence is the antithesis of a heroine's course. Remember, the best bad guys think they're doing it (whatever *it* is) for good reason. Sometimes they even *have* good reasons. They are just taking it too far in the wrong direction – wrong, in this context, will be anything that is diametrically opposed to the themes of the Heroine's Journey.

Obsession makes for wonderful enemies.

A well written bad guy behaves like a hero in the wrong journey, using people for his own concept of victory, rather than activating and supporting them as a network.

He may even be aligned with the heroine's needs... for a time.

CORRUPTING THE HEROINE FOR VILLAINY

Another twist on writing bad guys? Disguise your heroines as villains and your villains as heroines.

A corrupted heroine can also make for a fantastic enemy. Now that you have a better understanding of what makes a good heroine, you can understand what the precepts of her opposite would be: selfishness, violence, betrayal, loneliness.

A heroine can also be corrupted in that she is doing the right thing for the wrong reasons, or the wrong thing for the right reasons – kidnapping a child in pursuit of connection, for example. A heroine can be driven insane by having her networks broken, and she then may attempt to steal someone else's as a result. She hungers for connection so much that she takes that which belongs to others (lover, child, family, friend).

If she builds networks, only to sever them at the tiniest hint of betrayal, she's a great villain. If she sees her power in ruling over others and *telling* them what to do, or manipulating them into it, rather than asking them because she understands their strengths and delegates accordingly – she's a villain.

The same beats that make a heroine can be used to build a heroine as villain. Plus, this makes for an interesting foil.

Readers will sympathize with and understand her motives, because she is a reflection of what the heroine could become, had she a slightly different personality. Again, I am using gendered pronouns here, not referring to biological sex. A heroine corrupted can be male, female, nonbinary, or from an alien race with five genders, just like the heroine herself.

> Any step a heroine takes on her journey for the *right* reason, a villain can take for the *wrong* one.

If Demeter had responded to the discovery that Hades had raped Persephone by marching down and lopping off his head, she'd be a hero, not a heroine. Because the story would have been one of revenge, one of winning, one of who is stronger, not one of "How can we make this situation better?" It would still involve a withdrawal, and a descent, and a search, and a quest... just a corrupted version thereof.

- If the main character is driven into action not because she needs to repair what was broken, but because of revenge, a prevailing feeling that what has been done is hers to suffer alone, she is descending for the wrong reasons.
- If she responds to offers of aid by turning away, by isolating herself further, this will drive her toward evil.
- If her ultimate need is for dominance rather than solidarity, if her disguises and her manipulations are for solitary power and glory rather than for compromise and connection, she is a great enemy for our heroine.

She is not only the villain, but also a foil for readers to see how wrong a journey can go.

Seeing her go down at the end (probably under the weight of her own hubris) while the heroine lives on in the bosom of newfound family will be profoundly satisfying for readers.

DEFEAT OF THE VILLAIN

Which brings us nicely to the ways villains end in the context of a Heroine's Journey.

Yes, the villain can be killed or die, but that's often less satisfying to readers who prefer this narrative umbrella.

> I highly recommend considering themes of redemption rather than betrayal for your villains.

If we redeem bad or possibly evil characters through emotional connection, readers who prefer this journey will forgive a villain for his honest motivation. One example of this is Snape in the Harry Potter franchise. Everything bad that he did was for love of Harry's mother. Some of us forgive Snape because there is no greater motivation, so far as the Heroine's Journey is concerned, than love.

4

PUT SIDE CHARACTERS IN POWER

We've talked about goodies and baddies. Now I'd like to touch on the side characters, those who maybe only have one scene or a few lines of dialogue.

How can they be better applied to showcase a Heroine's Journey and please readers?

Well, these characters are way more important than you might think. What we have with them is what I like to call the *show me your doctor* moment.

That didn't make sense for this section's title, but still, that's the way I like to shout this out into the universe...

SHOW ME YOUR DOCTOR!

Every story is peopled not only with the main characters and their sidekicks or close companions or support cast (their family and friends), but also with more minor characters.

We might call these the *walk-on roles* or the *extras*. Some authors I know call them *throwaway characters*. Perhaps this character is an expert your detective consults about blood spatter, or the doctor your cop visits because of injury, a minor cousin at the manor house who runs the library, a professor of linguistics at a university.

These characters are there by necessity, more as plot devices than anything else. They exist to boost a scene, to drive narrative forward, or to convey integral information with the *voice of authority*.

> Yet they have tremendous power by virtue of their necessity.

In the Heroine's Journey, they carry particular significance because the transfer of information to a heroine is a key networking moment and therefore *vital* to her journey.

These voices of authority are often holders of in-world power in the context of the narrative: owners of property, political leaders, educators, healers, sorcerers, and the ultra-wealthy. While they may be on the page for only a limited time, they are vitally important to the effect on the world that you have as a narrator and the message that your fiction conveys to your audience.

I'm just going to go ahead and say it.

If you want to drive change toward a more inclusive narrative in general, and in the context of your universe in particular, these characters are *key*.

> Think *very very very* carefully about putting straight white able-bodied males into these power roles.

Why do I call this the *show me your doctor* moment?

We often, sadly, reach for the wise, grey-haired, avuncular Caucasian man when we write a doctor. This constantly puts only one type of person into a position of authority and knowledge (which is *power*, particularly for a heroine) in our books.

> The subtlety of checking our own instincts when portraying authority is vital.

Not only does it allow writers to somewhat control the messages we convey, it also gives us the opportunity to build a more complicated and interesting world for our characters to inhabit. Frankly, the straight white dude doctor? Sublimely boring. Yawn-fest.

CHARACTERS IN AUTHORITY

Want more reasons to think carefully about your side characters in these positions of power?

Complexity in authority has the added benefit of providing readers with a broader opportunity to recognize themselves (and their power possibilities) in print.

Also, you'll be building unique minor characters for them to latch onto. They will want to see more of these walk-on roles. They will write to you begging for backstory on that fantastic Peruvian lesbian jaguar shifter doctor you wrote. It colors your world with more interest. Frankly, it makes you less pat and dull as a creative voice.

The death knell to any writer is not "It was bad" or "I hated it," because at least you got an emotional reaction with those reviews. No, the death knell to a writer is, "It was boring." Because they won't bother to do anything more; they will just forget about you and your work forever.

> That's the career author's reason to think about your power player minor characters.

Considering *your doctor*, and who these characters are as whole people, is not just a way to exercise your creative muscle, it's a way to telegraph a message of real-world support into existence, to stop fear-mongering stereotypes (and bolstering prejudices), and to bring about subtle changes in the subconscious of an audience.

This is particularly vital when writing the Heroine's Journey because of the importance of her support network and the heightened value placed on information. The purveyor of useful intel is unlikely to betray our heroine. In fact, the heroine is more likely to absorb this new power player into her sphere, make them part of her network, and exhort them to her friends as a positive role model.

Thus, these voices of authority have immense power in what they give to the heroine and the narrative journey.

I encourage you to think carefully about how these side characters are described, what life they are given behind the scenes, and make certain none of us lean on straight, white, and male, merely because we are too lazy to come up with an alternative.

It's all in the details, and we storytellers must be particularly careful with our details when building characters. If they are powerful in the context of your book, then they are subversive in the context of your message. On the other hand, we can also unconsciously support a model of corruption and dominance.

You decide – it's your story.

I'm merely attempting to show you that you have the power to make that decision and that *you* may think it is a minor detail, but a thousand of these tiny choices can become a million representative moments.

And a million tiny examples in fiction?

That can change our perception of reality, for good or ill. That is, after all, the true power of narrative – normalization through empathy.

5

DIALOGUE IS YOUR FRIEND

The first four sections of this part were concerned with the power of character interactions.

Now I'm going to focus on how best to convey those interactions under the auspices of the Heroine's Journey. I've one word for you:

DIALOGUE

Dialogue is your friend. Conversations between characters establish connections and form the foundation of networks. The secret to making readers feel for characters, to really see them as vibrant and present, is dialogue.

I take great personal delight in grumpy or dour side characters.

Curmudgeons make for excellent comic relief and they are forgiven by readers for conveying necessary information because they can do so in a delightfully snarky or maudlin manner. I even made this character the hero of my first book, and boy, do readers love him.

The other extreme is exaggeration of the absurd as silly or snarky side character.

Again, one of my runaway popular side characters, Lord Akeldama, is a fabulous gay vampire who sparkles with diamonds and specializes in italicized diminutives. He's also a spy master. I've gotten more fan mail for him than any other character I have ever written. So much so, he started an advice column on my blog.

Both these personalities (the grumpy and the silly) are sublimely effective in dialogue. They tie nicely to the wise fool archetype. A character that is essentially ridiculous (in either direction) can surprise readers with a particularly perspicacious or profound observation entirely out of the blue and delivered in a funny manner. This can charm readers, provide for a twist not just in plot but in understanding, add new depth to character, plus offer up important information *and* deepen connections for our heroine.

A writerly win all round, if you ask me.

STRAIGHT MAN SYNDROME

One of the things I'd like to caution against is giving any one character *all* the good lines. Or always giving the best snark to your side characters.

Writers can fall into the habit of affection for one particularly shiny side character who, by virtue of having less page time, can nip in, be charming and funny and fabulous, and then flounce off. That character then becomes the most interesting part of a scene. Do this too many times in one book with the same character and this detracts from your main character.

You run the risk of straight-man syndrome (your main character becomes too normal and bland by contrast), particularly if you are writing lighter fare. Your protagonist becomes dull as a result of too much surrounding color. In other words, your main character also needs good lines. Don't forget her fair share of shine and sparkle – and a good way to ensure she has vibrancy is with her dialogue and voice.

Contemporary romance and other genres with modern settings will, generally speaking, rely on dialogue the most. Those genres that lean closer to Gothic tropes (such as *setting as character*), will need to describe the world and character more – like science fiction and fantasy. Other genres lean on the sidekick trope.

Cozy mysteries and buddy cop comedies, for example, almost always incorporate a sidekick. Some of this can be blamed on Sherlock Holmes, who popularized this technique, but another aspect is the importance of dialogue to convey clues and information in order to solve a crime. Conversational sidekicks serve a triple role – first to show the heroine in a constant act of networking and communication, second to convey information to the reader, and third to encourage expression of personality through dialogue.

I was asked once about how an author might sympathetically portray otherness (in this case, sexual identity) in print. There are plenty of good books, articles, and courses out there on this subject, but for me as a writer of the Heroine's Journey, it's usually done through dialogue.

Here's an example of my use of dialogue to convey a character's history, his coming out as queer experience (or not), and my own personal feelings on bisexual erasure. Tank is a large werewolf who also happens to be bisexual, and this conversation is between him and the man he has a crush on. Tank left his family to join a different werewolf pack because his previous one wasn't great about accepting gay members, but he never told them why.

> Tank said, "There's nine of us boys in the family."
>
> "All your size?"
>
> Tank laughed. "I'm pretty much the biggest, but they aren't that much smaller. Depeine males, the backbone of a pack. Together we basically form this big ol' defensive meat-wall."
>
> "That's a lot of family to leave behind."
>
> "There's enough of them to fill even a hole the size I left."
>
> "You didn't want to come out to them?"
>
> "I didn't."
>
> "Nice to be bi."
>
> "Easy to be invisible. Not quite the same thing."
>
> — G. L. CARRIGER (*THE OMEGA OBJECTION*)

WHY IS DIALOGUE SO EFFECTIVE?

The primary power in dialogue is that when written well, it is a tool to convey a great deal of information to an audience. The act of reading a back-and-forth conversation conveys *immediacy* and *relevance* to readers.

If you tend to write in third person, in particular, dialogue (in first person present tense) makes your readers feel more urgent as they inhabit the conversation themselves.

It's like they are eavesdropping on this back-and-forth in real time.

It's powerful because it is the most *present* part of your text. It encourages an instant emotional connection because the feeling when reading it is that it's happening *now*, compared to the surrounding third-person past narration. You can also use a character's internal thoughts to tap into this kind of immediacy.

6

LET HELP BE A STRENGTH

When writing this journey, one of the ways you have to show the intelligence and power of your main character is to have her identify problems for which the solution is another character's expertise. She has, after all, a network around her, and one of her primary skills is in activating it.

In this manner, writers can also show the capabilities and complementary abilities of other characters to each other, as well as to your heroine. This gives them added depth and complexity, which in turn broadens the accessibility of your universe.

> You can, because you are writing a Heroine's Journey, have side characters rescue your main character.

This is a fun way to twist an exciting scene or moment of drama – Ron finding the sword of Gryffindor for Harry is a great example. Hermione coming to Harry's rescue with yet another spell or vital piece of information is an ongoing use of this technique.

Remember that a heroine's notion of strength is in her contact with others. Which is not to say your heroine can't have unique abilities, can't be special herself – of course she can! But it should come as no surprise that Harry Potter is particularly good at team sports, should it?

This ties us back to the heroine's definition of success, which might incorporate defeating an enemy, but she doesn't have to do all of that defeating alone. Others can help her destroy her foe while she pursues the more important role of rebuilding and reunifying and connecting and negotiating for the good of all.

PORTION OUT ACHIEVEMENT

Another way to effectively write the Heroine's Journey is to portray resolution through portioning out achievement.

The heroine (and the reader) experiences joy in seeing glory shared as well as the glory itself. Giving accolades and praise or rewards for offers of information or assistance are hallmarks of a good heroine. She neither needs nor wants such things for herself, but is happy to dole them out.

In the Harry Potter franchise, Neville is not just another heroine and foil for Harry, he is there to take on part of Harry's burden and duty, and part of the glory. Neville is, to a certain extent, the Horus to Harry's Isis. Interestingly, he acts as a minor obstacle in the first Harry Potter book – when he attempts to stop Harry and his friends from undertaking their descent and search. He is, amusingly enough, rewarded for this with the praise and accolades needed to win the House Cup. Portioning out achievement indeed! It is Neville who stays behind and fights for the school in the later books (his home and network), and it is Neville who will take out the final horcrux (the snake) with a sword.

How very Horus versus Set!

As readers of this narrative, we love and support Neville in this role, first because he is so important to the plot and second because he is so important to the Heroine's Journey. He is capable of action and of growing into his courage in order to assist Harry on his journey, but he is also engaging in his own version of this journey and developing into a more complex and strong character as a result.

This kind of tactic resonates with readers of this journey because it ties to the sense of community that many of them are hungry to read as part of this narrative.

Also, it showcases that the outsider, the geek, the outcast also has a place and a function and can become a plot pivot. Readers want to see their heroine sharing burdens, but they also want her to share her rewards and victories.

It is far better to celebrate with others than alone.

In fact, there is no celebration at all if there isn't a network to bolster positive outcomes. Because she could not complete her journey without other people, a good heroine realizes this and praises others, and a good writer of the journey shows that on the page.

GIVE YOUR CHARACTERS HUMOR

Remember Iambe in the Demeter myth?

She too is important when writing the Heroine's Journey. If you're writing this narrative and can't face tackling full-on comedy, at least go for a few moments of levity. Humor is a tool for many things – pacing, primarily, but also access to connecting emotionally with your readers.

Never doubt that it is incredibly hard to write funny, but if you can manage it, my goodness, will you cultivate dedicated fans.

COMEDY AND TENSION

The act of making a reader laugh (much like making them cry) can break down their guarded defense against the immersive experience. It frees the writer to activate intimate access to your reader's psyche.

If you have surprised them enough to make them laugh, they are, for a split second at least, cracked open to your emotional manipulation.

Laughing affects a reader's heart rate, so you can use the moment after amusement to relax them before delivering a narrative punch, which by comparison makes the punch more powerful. (*I am a leaf on the wind*, anyone?)

You can also do the opposite of this, break up a hot sex scene with farce, a powerfully sad funeral with levity, or a fight scene with snark, intentionally getting you readers to relax before you make them tense again. You can always inject a ready quip to intentionally break tension, giving your reader some breathing room. We see this all the time in the James Bond franchise.

Yes, I know, this seems cold. But what are we writers but Machiavellian manipulators of a stranger's emotions?

Isn't that why we write – to cause other humans to feel and to think?

Moments of levity and humor are shockingly effective at breaking tension in calculated ways.

COMEDY AND PACE

From a purely craft perspective, applying humor is also effective.

Readers will forgive a lot if you make them smile, including such things as extended openings, info-dumps, descriptions, slow action-less scenes, red herrings, and romantic moments. In this way comedy helps with story pacing.

Authors can develop a sing-song voice that includes things like sentence and paragraph structure, length of words, and the order in which they follow each other. This accidental structure can lull readers into listlessness. You can wake them up with a shake of laughter, and suddenly they will pay very close attention to the text following.

> In this way, comedy can also be a tool for grabbing reader focus.

COMEDY AND INFORMATION

Comedy, comedic dialogue, and comedic characters are means by which an author can delicately deliver information to readers – information about other characters, plot, and world building, yes, but also profound messages of hope and change.

As one of my most popular (and most ridiculous) side characters, Ivy Hisselpenny, puts it:

> "The great advantage," she said, "of being thought silly, is that people forget and begin to think one might also be foolish. I may, Professor Lyall, be a trifle enthusiastic in my manners and dress, but I am no fool."

> — GAIL CARRIGER (*BLAMELESS*)

It's a fantastic tool in your bag of authorial tricks. Not only can you deliver one-two punches of revelation, psychological connection, or emotional manipulation using humor, you can also bring about societal normalization. Comedy can normalize alternate models of life, love, or even culture – by fair means, not foul.

HUMOR IS SUBVERSIVE

The Heroine's Journey, because of its leaning toward dialogue and connection, naturally encourages humor as part of its arsenal, and I encourage you to make use of this powerful tool.

Which brings us to the risk you take when including humor.

It's unlikely that you, or your books, will be taken seriously if they are defined primarily as *funny*. But if you're writing the Heroine's Journey, that's already a risk.

Because comedy is easily dismissed, it's all too easily underestimated as well.

This make it very subversive.

USE GOTHIC TROPES TO INDICATE GENRE

Use the Gothic tropes to nest your Heroine's Journey into the right genre and subgenre, one that suits both the journey and the story.

This way, readers know what to expect from you and your work and are left with an additional sense of satisfaction.

Reading the *right* book that has been categorized in the *right* way provides an additional sense of comfort to readers.

Remember, readers of the Heroine's journey in particular are looking for comfort from their stories. Using tropes to seat your narrative in the perfect niche is good for everyone concerned because that, like the story, will provide a lingering sense of joy and satisfaction.

So that's why I wrote that whole section on the Gothics.

USE GOTHIC ARCHETYPES TO SURPRISE READERS

On the flip side, you can use Gothic archetypes to surprise your readers with new twists on old characters in the context of a Heroine's Journey. This will add to sensations of joy and excitement as they read, plus give them side characters to identify with or wish to learn more about.

They will be *pleasantly* surprised if you are thoughtful in your application of these archetypes, and you'd better control for any negative messaging, which can undermine the quality of your work.

Okay, so those are your ten best tools for writing the Heroine's Journey in the modern age.

A COUNSELING SESSION

In which I turn into a bit of a counselor – for which I am, I assure you, entirely unqualified

And now, a brief word on writerly health.

As I discussed in **Chapter 6**, the Heroine's Journey as it now stands in society is profoundly critically and culturally devalued by the modern western world. This is endemic to our society, yet if you write these journeys, in these subgenres, chances are you are going to get flak for it.

> Try owning up to being a romance author at your average cocktail party.

Probably doesn't sound like a lot of fun, does it?

Sure, it might be a bit better now than it once was, but even owning up to writing genre fiction can be a social risk under the confines of nonwriter society.

Here's the only thing we who write this narrative can do.

Stop worrying about being labeled as soft, sentimental, fluffy, or frivolous because we write the Heroine's Journey.

It's hard to explain to your average Joe the Sausage Seller why this narrative is important.

Look at me – I ended up having to write a whole flipping book about it.

> But like writing comedy, the true secret is that this narrative is profoundly powerful and profitable.

It doesn't really matter what people think (loudly, in public), because as the huge number of romance readers can attest, it will not impact your audience reach. We will survive despite mockery at cocktail parties.

If you leave readers with a sense of community and feeling happy? They will love you forever regardless of label. And readers will find you, because so many of us are in ever greater need of comfort.

CONNECTION MEANS CAREER

Once, very early on in my career, I was up for an award in the SF/F field. I lost (rather badly, as it turns out). I wasn't that upset, honestly, because I figured writing SF/F with a strong romance thread and lots of humor wasn't ever going to win me awards. There were three major strikes against me, after all – comedy, romance, and the Heroine's Journey. Doomed never to be taken seriously.

> Dooomed, I say!

And now, of course, I'm hoping you better understand why.

I'm not trolling for sympathy. This is merely to say I was sitting at the bar later that night, after having lost, and my publisher sidled up to me to tender his sympathy.

"Sorry you didn't win," said he.

I grinned at him and replied, "You know, I'll take the bestseller list any day." And I meant it.

He clinked his glass to mine and we talked of other things.

If you write the Heroine's Journey, you're providing comfort and connection with your words. This is like sending a story out into the world that is a virtual hug.

What happens, if you do this well, is that fans will see you, the storyteller, as an instrument of *their* comfort and sensation of connection.

What you'll hopefully end up with is rabid fans, because they naturally transfer this sensation to you, their author. They love you, because they love your voice, and they love your voice because you're activating a deeply held ancient narrative promoting love and unity and family.

In a way, your books will do what they tell.

They will create community.

If you're lucky, they will even build you a support network of readers. To the best of those fans, this means they give back, and support you. It's the exact model you have shown them in the context of the Heroine's Journey narrative.

What that means in the long run is a lifelong career as a storyteller.

BE THE HEROINE

Why we need a second journey

One of the things I hope I've established with this book is that when we consider both the Heroine's Journey and the Hero's Journey as narratives, the *purpose* of the story becomes a key distinguishing feature.

> We love the Hero's Journey because it is about striving, conquering, and victorious power.

The hero succeeds against all odds. His heroism is vested in his ability to accomplish what is asked of him by himself, despite interference.

> We love the Heroine's Journey because it is about defeating adversity through connection and recognition of others' abilities.

It is about the courage to ask for help, because asking for help is not a weakness. In fact, the heroine's very ability to do so is her most enduring strength.

Heroines are deities and parents, spouses and lovers, men and women and nonbinary folk. Heroines are hunting for what was taken from them. This also makes them leaders, generals, strategists, and planners. Connection to others is not a failing, it is the source of their power. Heroines are in the most danger when they are isolated. Heroines do not want revenge or to strive alone against all comers. They want family.

I'm going to say this one last time because it is a concept so alien to the modern world.

A heroine not only asks for help, she is good at it. She learns how to ask the right people, and to embrace both them and their advice.

> For a heroine, asking for help is *not a weakness*, it is profoundly empowering.

There is no shame in storytellers employing either narrative.

There is shame when an entire culture of storytellers and critics values one narrative over the other. I believe that culturewide damage is done if we, as a whole, tout one journey as better, or more powerful, or more appealing than the other.

When we do that, tragedy results... in all senses of the word.

For example, if the Hero's Journey defines what it means to be *strong* because we've decided, culturally, that readers enjoy that journey more and have been trained to see it everywhere, our societal concept of a powerful female character becomes a biological woman behaving in a hyper-heroic way (e.g. violent, isolated, physically powerful).

What I hope you have learned from this book more than anything else, is to question that bias.

> To realize, in fact, that it is not our idea of what it means to be *female* that should be critically examined under these circumstances, but instead, our idea of what it means to be *strong*.

IT'S OUR RESPONSIBILITY

We who write fiction are the custodians of narrative.

We want to tell our stories. We *need* to tell our stories. And people need and want to read them.

Let us please never forget how very powerful those stories are as a result of that need.

After everything is said and done, we write because we must. But we *publish* and we put our stories out there into the world because we are hungry for connection. We desire to find our readers. Our audience.

Our family.

What is our story then but a cry sent into the universe asking for a network of comfort and support?

Who are we but heroines in our own way?

So please, go forth.

Write.

Be a heroine.

EPILOGUE

In which I encounter a Twitter troll and am forced to justify my existence

When I tweeted that I was going to write a book about the Heroine's Journey, I was immediately trolled.

Essentially the dudebro said the following:

How are you qualified to write that?

My instinctive reactions were exactly what you might expect. They ranged from disheartened impostor syndrome to snarky rebuttal to defensively angry to academically pedantic.

Disheartened:

How am I qualified? Oh no. What am I doing? What's my purpose in life?

Snarky:

Because I am a heroine – I get up every day, drink tea, and have to deal with dudes like you on the internet.

Defensive:

> *Two master's degrees, thirteen New York Times bestsellers, and over a million books in print. How are you qualified to talk to me?*

Academic:

> *The fact that you feel justified in asking that question while knowing nothing about me exemplifies the entrenched nature of the Hero's Journey – confront instead of collaborate, react to offers of information with suspicion, self-defend instead of engage with openness.*

I tweeted none of these things. I ignored him. Because if a decade of writing books in the Internet age has taught me nothing else, it's this:

> Don't read bad reviews and don't engage with trolls.

Honestly?

I am no more qualified to write a nonfiction book on the Heroine's Journey, academically speaking, than you are. The only social proof I have to offer is a bunch of best-selling fiction books and the fact that every single one of them uses the Heroine's Journey as a chassis.

Perhaps a more qualified academic will come along and provide the Heroine's Journey analysis that storytellers have been hoping for. Until then, you're stuck with me, a leaking plug for the hole of intellectual absence.

Yuck.

That analogy just got away from me.

You know what I'm trying to say.

If you feel more qualified to write this book, or think you can do better, please do. More books are vital. Always. I am begging for more books, more thoughts, more works on the Heroine's Journey.

If you know of other myths or legends or fairy stories that fit this model of the Heroine's Journey, or don't fit it, then please write about them, blog about them, talk about them, discuss them.

These are neglected stories and we must do everything we can to revive them, to make them known again, to talk about them and how they have affected us and our own works of fiction.

Until then, I needed to write this because there is a mighty need for a better understanding of, affection for, and defense of the Heroine's Journey.

> My mother always told me that *she who sees the problem is responsible for the solution.*

This book, I suppose, is my personal version of a Heroine's Journey – one of networking and understanding, and yes, even compromise.

You see, I would like to have waited. I would like to have delegated (as a good heroine should). Instead, I kept waiting and lamenting the lack and the loss. I kept noticing the descent into afterlife and madness, and I knew there must be a search, and a gathering of information, and an understanding, and a dissemination of that understanding. The responsibility has fallen upon me whether I like it or not.

I hope this helps, and I really hope it is for the good of us all. Because one of the keys to the Heroine's Journey is that we do this together, because therein lies our strength.

So, thank you for reading this and journeys like it. For loving authors and supporting them. Thank you for writing and consuming the Heroine's Journey.

We fight by networking, so please find me online, or drop me a line via my website, join my newsletter the Chirrup, or write a review... or go off and do it for some other author you love.

Be kind to yourself and to others.

Support.

Solidarity.

Comfort.

CITATIONS & REFERENCES EXPLAINED

I intentionally chose not to write my references as footnotes or endnotes, because frankly, that kinda sucks in these days of ebooks.

Instead, I have broken these down into two sections. I'm trying to make them fun enough that you read even this bit.

CITATIONS

Citations include those documents, archaeological fragments, and publications that I refer to in focused detail and directly quote in this book.

- First, I've structured the citation as it actually appears in the text.
- Then I've included a few additional notes so that you better understand why I chose it.

Hopefully, this makes it easy to find if you want to read more (and to check my work or draw your own conclusions).

Because I read stuff both on paper and electronically, some of my direct citation points are LOC. This is a location code, the digital version of a page number. Because digital content can be reformatted, page numbers are flexible and consequently meaningless in digital. LOC is based on a percentage completed of the total word count in a book.

REFERENCES

In the second section, *References*, I did encyclopedia-style blurbs for the pop culture stuff I talk about in the books, which is listed by franchise/common name or title.

I've included information I feel is relevant to this book, and I'm being sublimely flippant.

CITATIONS

Anonymous critic. (1966) "Extracting Emily," *Time*, 22 April 1966.

Budge, E. A. Wallis. (1911) *Osiris and the Egyptian resurrection.* (Digital source so referenced by LOC #). Sir Ernest Alfred Thompson Wallis Budge (1857–1934) is widely considered the father of Egyptology in the UK. His work is colored by a conflation of opinion and fact, biased Victorian notions of how the universe worked, and a telling belief in the occult. However, his translations of Egyptian myth had great impact on western culture at the time, and therefore on any resulting societywide knowledge of these myths that resulted.

Budge, Ernest Alfred Wallis. (1960) *The Book of the Dead: The Hieroglyphic Transcript of the Papyrus of ANI, the Translation into English and Introduction by E. Wallis Budge, Late Keeper of the Egyptian and Assyrian Antiquities in The British Museum.* Bell Publishing, New York. I'm particularly interested in Budge's English translation of a hieroglyphic text that was first translated into French in 1879 in *Les monuments égyptiens de la Bibliothèque nationale, Plates XXI-XXVII,* Paris.

Budge, Ernest Alfred Wallis. (1895) Original publication of *The Book of the Dead* is in the public domain and available online via this redirect gailcarriger.com/HJ_Budge1895

Burkert, Walter. (1985) *Greek Religion.* Harvard University Press. Comprehensive guide with secondary references to the Demeter myth, first published in German in 1977. Uses archaeological evidence, ancient philosophies on the subject, and Linear B inscriptions (amongst other things) to reconstruct religious beliefs, rituals, festivals, temples, practitioners, and cults of the Minoan-Mycenaean age. Attention is paid to contested academic analysis and parts of the historical record that are still opaque.

Carpenter, Julia. (2019) "Romance Novelists Write About Sex and Pleasure. On the Internet That Makes Them Targets for Abuse" article for *Glamour Magazine* online June 25, 2019. Available online via this redirect: gailcarriger.com/HJ_Carpenter

Campbell, Joseph. (1949) *The Hero with a Thousand Faces.* Published by the Bollingen Foundation through Pantheon Press. A work of comparative mythology describing the journey of the hero (as archetype) found in various myths and Campbell's theory behind its structure. His analysis relied on Freudian concepts, Jungian archetypes, unconscious forces, and rites of passage rituals (e.g., Arnold van Gennep's *Separation, Initiation and Return*).

Corelli, Marie. (1855–1924) English novelist and literary success (1886 through World War I) who wrote hugely popular Gothic-influenced romance novels that also incorporated occultism, mystery, and Christian morality. She has been largely ignored by history and literary critics, despite the fact that at the time she roundly outsold her male counterparts.

Homer. *Homeric Hymn to Demeter* translated by Gregory Nagy (no date given). Center for Hellenic Studies, Harvard University. One of the most commonly used translations of this myth. Made available online via Harvard University via this redirect: gailcarriger.com/HJ_Nagy

Larsen, Stephen and Robin Larsen. (2002) *Joseph Campbell: A Fire in the Mind*. Inner Traditions. The authorized biography of Joseph Campbell covers his life and a personal perspective through the voices of friends and colleagues. Written by two of Campbell's students who had access to his notes and journals.

Murdock, Maureen. (1990) *Heroine's Journey: Woman's Quest for Wholeness*. Shambhala Publications. A student of Joseph Campbell, Murdock published *The Heroine's Journey* partly as riposte to his *Hero with a Thousand Faces*. Murdock, a Jungian therapist, saw the Heroine's Journey as primarily a therapeutic process in a search for the whole self, the story format of which remained structurally similar to the Hero's. More can be found online, here's a redirect: gailcarriger.com/HJ_Murdock

Plutarch. (1936 translation by F. C. Babbitt) *De Iside et Osiride and Moralia. Vol. v: Isis and Osiris* (transl.) London and Cambridge, MA. Can also be found online as *Plutarch's Morals, Theosophical Essays, Isis's quest, section 18* translated by Charles William King (1908). More can be found online, here's a redirect: gailcarriger.com/HJ_Plutarch

Rogers, Deborah D. (1994, editor) *The Critical Responses to Ann Radcliffe*. Greenwood Press, Connecticut and London. Collection of historically documented opinion and critical review of Radcliffe and her work during and just after her lifetime, plus modern essays and analysis. Seems somewhat positively biased and intentionally avoids negative reviews.

Radcliffe, Ann. (1764–1823) English author and pioneer of Gothic fiction, the most popular writer of her day and highest paid writer of the 1790s. Her best-known work is *The Mysteries of Udolpho* (1794) later parodied by Jane Austen in *Northanger Abbey* (1817). She influenced a generation of romantic authors who would eventually spawn the romance genre as we know it today.

Schmidt, Victoria Lynn. (2001) *45 Master Characters: Mythic Models for Creating Original Characters*. Writer's Digest Books. Draws strongly on both myth and fairy tale foundations to analyze character archetypes and discusses Inanna and the Heroine's Journey.

Scott, William Stuart. (1955) *Marie Corelli: The Story of a Friendship*. Hutchinson, London.

Siculus, Diodorus. (1933 translation by C. H. Oldfather) *Library of History: Book 1*. London and New York.

Shaw, Garry J. (2014) *The Egyptian Myths*. Thames & Hudson. Secondary source gathering multiple Egyptian myths; care is given to source and conflicting accounts.

Watt, Ian. (1957) *The Rise of the Novel: Studies in Defoe, Richardson, and Fielding*. Los Angeles and Berkeley, University of California Press.

Wolkstein, Diane and Kramer, Samuel Noah. (1993) *Inanna: Queen of Heaven and Earth.* Harper & Row. Compilation of translated archaeological fragments plus essays on interpretation from multiple authors. Based on evidence collected by two separate universities around the turn of the century.

REFERENCES

Batman character. Superhero character from DC Comics, created by artist Bob Kane and writer Bill Finger. He first appeared in *Detective Comics* #27 in 1939, he's had a live action kid-focused TV show (1966–1968), as well as animated TV series, multiple movies, and video game adaptations over the years.

> Gail's assessment: Usually portrayed as a classic Byronic hero.

Battlestar Galactica TV series. (2004–2009) Science fiction TV series space opera developed by Ronald D. Moore. A reboot of the 1978 *Battlestar Galactica* TV series created by Glen A. Larson.

> Gail's thoughts: Notorious for its popularity at the time, yet criticized for a shabby final season. I believe this is partly the result of a conflict between Heroine's and Hero's Journeys.

Black Panther movie. (2018) Superhero film based on the Marvel Comics character of the same name. It's technically an origin story, although it doesn't have the typical tropes one expects of discovery and self-expression.

> Gail's analysis: This movie has elements of a Hero's Journey in that victory is nested in an expression of physical violence and defeat of an enemy one on one. There is also the dead father/mentor figure and death (not once but twice). On the other hand, it has Heroine's Journey tropes as well in that loss of allies and isolation results in risk and near death; help is required to revive the main character; the allies who search are family (mother, sister, lover); Black Panther's strength is reborn through networking; and he trusts in his friends to defend him. Also, the movie has lots of elements of group action, infiltration, exchange of useful information, and spying (particularly in the first half) – the hallmarks of a caper. *Black Panther* ends with community outreach, but the final shot is solitary. To top it all off, the male fighters are given defensive supernatural abilities, the women offensive. Honestly, I'm including it here because it was so confusing and I want to at least give voice to that. An example of a successful work of popular culture that, in the end, uses neither the Hero's nor the Heroine's Journey as its solo chassis. Remarkable.

Captain Marvel movie. (2019) Superhero film based on a Marvel Comics character of the same name written and directed by Anna Boden and Ryan Fleck.

> Gail's analysis: Buddy cop comedy meets Heroine's Journey.

Children of the Corn book by Stephen King. (1977) A short horror story first published in *Penthouse* magazine, and later collected in *Night Shift* (1978). Turned into a film (1984) by New World Pictures, and then a franchise (1992–2018), remade for TV in 2009 by Fox 21 Television for the Syfy network.

Gail's reaction: Scary.

CSI: Crime Scene Investigation TV series. (2000–2015) Procedural investigative crime drama TV series that aired on CBS for fifteen seasons.

Gail's thoughts: Example of a hero leading a group in a Heroine's Journey and changing into a heroine over time.

Dangerous Liaisons movie. (1988) Period-set dramatic film written by Christopher Hampton as an adaptation of the 18th-century French epistolary novel *Les liaisons dangereuses* by Pierre Choderlos de Laclos. This original work is so iconic it has been adapted into plays, operas, ballets, and seven films: *Les Liaisons dangereuses* (1959), *Une femme fidèle* (1976), *Dangerous Liaisons* (1988 – my favorite), *Valmont* (1989), *Cruel Intentions* (1999), *Untold Scandal* (2003), and *Dangerous Liaisons* (2012).

Gail's assessment: Excellent example of repackaging Gothic archetypes into a historical melodrama.

Deadpool movie. (2016) Superhero film based on the Marvel Comics character of the same name with a screenplay by Rhett Reese and Paul Wernick.

Gail's thoughts: Deadpool is a classic Byronic antihero on an even more classic Hero's Journey. That lovely girlfriend was never gonna make it.

Die Hard movie. (1988) Action thriller film with screenplay by Steven E. de Souza and Jeb Stuart (based on Roderick Thorp's 1979 novel *Nothing Lasts Forever*).

Gail's analysis: Iconic example of the Hero's Journey and destined to define the beats of trapped location suspense and disaster storylines.

The Divergent Series (book series 2011–2013) and movies (film series 2014–2016). Three YA dystopian science fiction adventure novels (*Divergent*, *Insurgent*, and *Allegiant*) by Veronica Roth, turned into three feature films of the same names.

Gail's assessment: The main character, Tris, engages in a tragic Hero's Journey that ends with her death as an act of self-sacrifice and was polarizing for readers. Could be seen as a tragic Heroine's Journey, depending on analysis, which might explain some readers' sense of betrayal.

Dune franchise. Science fiction space opera franchise originating with the novel *Dune* by Frank Herbert (1965). *Dune* is arguably the bestselling science fiction book of all time, and has been adapted into films (1984 and 2020), TV miniseries (2000), and games.

Gail's thoughts: The books employ multiple POVs and many narrative elements of the classic Hero's Journey.

ER TV series. (1994–2009) Medical drama TV series (with procedural elements) created by novelist and doctor Michael Crichton that aired on NBC.

> Gail's analysis: Example of different heroes and heroines leading a group in what is most likely a Heroine's Journey. Hard to define *successful outcome* with something this long running.

The Expanse TV series. (2015 ongoing) Science fiction political space opera TV series based on *The Expanse* novels by James S. A. Corey.

> Gail's thoughts: Example of a multiple-POV narrative featuring different heroes and heroines on what could be either a Hero's or Heroine's Journey chassis. Hard to tell without knowing the ending.

Firefly TV series. (2002–2003) Space opera meets Western TV series, created by writer, director, and executive producer Joss Whedon, under his Mutant Enemy Productions label.

> Gail's analysis: Cancelled early, but when taken into consideration along with the follow-up movie, *Serenity* (2005), this most likely has a Heroine's Journey chassis.

Game of Thrones TV series. (2011–2019) Epic fantasy TV series that aired on HBO created by David Benioff and D. B. Weiss. Adaptation of *A Song of Ice and Fire* series by George R. R. Martin, multiple-POV politically driven epic fantasy series. Widely believed to be based on various historical events, including the Wars of the Roses.

Gail's note: The book series was unfinished at the time of this writing, but the TV show gives some insight into journey patterns and intent. This is an example of a multiple-POV narrative featuring different heroes and heroines on what is arguably a Hero's Journey chassis.

Girls Trip movie. 2017 comedy film directed by Malcolm D. Lee and focused on travel and female friendship.

Gail's note: This movie depicts power in groups in the form of female friendship and platonic relationships as well as heterosexual romances with men. It's a Heroine's Journey.

Harry Potter character. The titular character in the Harry Potter books by J. K. Rowling, 1997–2007. There are seven books in the series, the first of which is *Harry Potter and the Philosopher's Stone*. There are eight movie adaptations (2001–2011) that follow the same narrative arc. In the text, I usually refer to this collective of both books and movies as *the Harry Potter franchise*.

Gail's thoughts: I use this as an example of the Heroine's Journey for a reason.

House M.D. AKA *House* TV series. (2004–2012) TV medical drama on the Fox network featuring Dr. Gregory House, a medical genius who leads a diagnostic hospital team.

Gail's assessment: This is a doctor version of Sherlock Holmes on a medical procedure chassis. (Yeah, his tolerant BFF is named Wilson… I see what you did there.) Exactly like Holmes, House is clearly a hero, but because of the waffling nature of a long-running procedural without overarching story, it's nearly impossible (and basically unnecessary) to apply a journey chassis to this show.

The Hunger Games trilogy (books 2008–2010) and *The Hunger Games* movies (film series). Three YA dystopian science fiction adventure novels: *The Hunger Games* (2008), *Catching Fire* (2009), and *Mockingjay* (2010) by Suzanne Collins, turned into four feature films of the same names (the third book split into two parts).

> Gail's assessment: The main character, Katniss Everdeen, engages in a Heroine's Journey that includes many tropes and archetypes endemic to the journey and to coming of age YA narratives. These include love triangles and themes of partnership, delegation, and redemption. The initial prompting for her actions is the threatened removal of her sister, Primrose.

Iliad poem. Ancient Greek epic poem attributed to Homer, set during the Trojan War.

> Gail's note: Features the ultimate emo hero Achilles and his BFF/lover/foil Patroclus.

James Bond character. (1953 ongoing) Iconic example of a hero within the spy suspense genre, includes books, movies, radio plays, comics, TV shows, video games, and more. All of these focus on fictional British Secret Service agent James Bond, created by author Ian Fleming. Fleming wrote twelve Bond novels and two short-story collections. After his death (1964) eight other authors picked up the torch (or should I say, gun?). The Bond movies (of which there are 26) form the longest continually running film series in history.

> Gail's note: Bond is a classic, even archetypical, hero.

Jack Reacher character. (1997) Fictional character in thriller suspense books written by Lee Child, at a rate of approximately one per year since 1997. Main character is a former American military policeman who wanders (mostly) the United States taking odd jobs, investigating suspicious activities, and getting into danger. Adapted into two movies (2012, 2016) starring Tom Cruise.

> Gail's analysis: Wildly popular example of a hero on Heroic Journeys within the thriller genre, where he usually fits nicely.

Jeeves character. (1915–1974) Fictional character in a series of comedic novels and short stories by P. G. Wodehouse adapted to film and stage on multiple occasions. Has entered the cultural lexicon as a word used to mean butler or servant.

> Gail's thoughts: Jeeves is the brilliant, competent valet of wealthy, idle imbecile Bertie Wooster. He spends his time saving Wooster and his equally idiotic friends from a series of relationships and other scrapes. He is a perfect example of the wise servant archetype.

Law & Order TV series. (1990–2010) Police procedural meets legal drama TV series created by Dick Wolf that aired on NBC and ran for twenty seasons.

Gail's analysis: Carries similar issues as other long-running procedurals like *House M.D.*, *ER*, and *CSI* in terms of analysis of story journey (when there really isn't one over the long haul), although we can spot hero and heroine archetypes at play.

The Lord of the Rings book. (1937) High fantasy novel in three volumes written (1937–1949) by J. R. R. Tolkien, turned into movies (2001–2003) as three films: *The Fellowship of the Ring* (2001), *The Two Towers* (2002), and *The Return of the King* (2003). One of the most popular books of its day. Tolkien is widely regarded as the father of high fantasy.

Gail's thoughts: There is a lot of Tolkien analysis out there; this book/series is multiple-POV and complex, but comprises multiple heroes (and a few heroines) on various journeys, one of the hallmarks of broad-scope fantasy.

Leverage TV series. (2008–2012) Heist/caper drama TV series with a comedic bent.

Gail's feels: I adore this show. It follows a five-person antihero team and uses a Robin Hood narrative device. It's multiple POVs but does have an underlying sort-of story that strongly indicates Heroine's Journey.

Love, Simon movie. (2018) Romantic teen comedy-drama written by Isaac Aptaker and Elizabeth Berger, and based on the YA book *Simon vs. the Homo Sapiens Agenda* by Becky Albertalli (2015).

Gail's thoughts: Good example of a well-executed Heroine's Journey in a modern setting with standard teen romance tropes in play.

Men in Black movie. (1997) Science-fiction buddy cop comedy film written by Ed Solomon. Titular characters are tasked with supervising extraterrestrial life on Earth, based on a comic book series of the same name, but which had a much different tone.

Gail's thoughts: Iconic combination of science fiction and buddy comedy featuring one hero and one heroine on a Heroine's Journey chassis.

Sherlock Holmes character. (1887) The titular character of many books, movies, and TV shows. Arguably the world's best-known fictional detective. Invented by Sir Arthur Conan Doyle, first appearing in print in 1887. Doyle is often talked of as the father of cozy mysteries, with Agatha Christie as the mother.

Gail's analysis: Most Holmes mysteries are told by his roommate Watson using a frame narrative technique and activating the *explanatory sidekick* plot device.

Spider-Man character. (1962) Superhero character from Marvel Comics created by writer-editor Stan Lee and writer-artist Steve Ditko in *Amazing Fantasy* #15 (1962). He's had a number of movies, television shows, and video game adaptations.

Gail's thoughts: Possibly the primary example of a YA coming-of-age narrative in the comic book world.

Spider-Man: Into the Spider-Verse movie. (2018) Animated superhero film featuring the Miles Morales version of Spider-Man.

> Gail's thoughts: Typical example of a coming-of-age Hero's Journey YA narrative (AKA the action version of the emotional, psychological, and moral journey undertaken in most *Bildungsroman*). Includes multiple friend/mentor characters, evil uncle, violent victory in one-on-one combat, and results in typical messages of finding inner strength and the burden of adult responsibility.

Star Trek: The Original Series TV series. (1966–1967) Science fiction TV series created by Gene Roddenberry.

> Gail's analysis: Mainly a buddy comedy/drama only with one hero and two foils (Bones representing the feminine, and Spock the wise fool archetype). Series was canceled but also was distinctly episodic, so difficult to tell which journey was ultimately intended.

Star Trek: The Next Generation TV series. (1987–1994) Space opera TV series created by Gene Roddenberry and featuring an ensemble cast.

> Gail's thoughts: Egalitarian follow-up series to *Star Trek: The Original Series* with the captain as more of a delegating character. The TV series (at least) appears to be a Heroine's Journey.

Star Wars movie. (1977) AKA *Star Wars original* or *Star Wars: Episode IV – A New Hope*. Science fiction film written and directed by George Lucas, and the first film in the original *Star Wars* trilogy, followed by *The Empire Strikes Back* (1980) and *Return of the Jedi* (1983).

> Gail's note: Widely known as an intentional representation of the Hero's Journey.

Star Wars prequel movie. (1999) AKA *Star Wars: Episode I – The Phantom Menace*. Science fiction film written and directed by George Lucas, and the first film in the second *Star Wars* trilogy, followed by *Attack of the Clones* (2002) and *Revenge of the Sith* (2005).

> Gail's note: I honestly don't have much to say about these except that, for various reasons, they are pretty roundly vilified.

Supergirl TV series. (2015 ongoing). Superhero TV series based on the DC Comic book character Supergirl (created by Otto Binder and Al Plastino) and set in the Arrowverse franchise.

> Gail's thoughts: As of this writing, the series still seems to be mainly a classic Heroine's Journey.

To All the Boys I've Loved Before book (2014) and movie (2018). Text refers to both the 2014 YA romance novel by Jenny Han and the 2018 film directed by Susan Johnson.

> Gail's analysis: A Heroine's Journey and classic romantic teen comedy that employs many of the tropes and archetypes of the YA romance genre: fake boyfriend, secret crush, miscommunication and reconciliation, complicated family dynamics, dead parent, public humiliation, self-discovery, and coming of age.

The Twilight Saga movie franchise and book series. (2005) Text refers to the four romantic fantasy YA novels by Stephenie Meyer (2005–2008) and the five adapted films from Summit Entertainment (2009–2012). The individual titles are *Twilight, New Moon, Eclipse,* and *Breaking Dawn* (this last was broken into two parts for the movies.)

> Gail's note: This franchise is a Heroine's Journey and was hugely commercially successful.

Waiting to Exhale book and movie. (1992) Text refers to both the 1992 novel by Terry McMillan and the 1995 film directed by Forest Whitaker.

> Gail's note: Both book and film depict power in female friendships and platonic relationships as well as, and in some cases instead of, heterosexual romance. It's a Heroine's Journey.

Wolverine character. (1974) Fictional antihero superhero from Marvel Comics first appearing in print in 1974, created by Roy Thomas, Len Wein, and John Romita Sr. and drawn for publication by Herb Trimpe. Wolverine has appeared in animated TV series, video games, and films.

> Gail's thoughts: Possibly the best well-known iteration of a Byronic hero in modern times.

Wonder Woman movie. (2017) Superhero film from a screenplay by Allan Heinberg, based on the DC Comics character of the same name.

> Gail's note: One of the best recent examples of a classic Hero's Journey.

AKNOWLEDGEMENTS

My most profound gratitude to the most wonderful group of early readers anyone could ask for. Thank you for taking time out of your busy lives and away from your amazing manuscripts to help me with mine.

You are my heroines: Asa Maria Bradley, Lauren Harris, Piper J. Drake, Tess Rider, Stephanie Burgis, Ryvenna Altman, Kristin Nelson, Angelica R. Jackson, Christina Boekeloo, Ty, Josh Storey, Marissa Priest, Lea Kirk, and J. Daniel Sawyer.

And to my second pass stalwarts who had much less time and still did their best, Lisa Root, Tanya J. Nielsen, and Janis.

Thanks to my local romance writer's collective, *Locus Magazine*, and Bronwyn Emory, who let me test the Heroine's Journey as a presentation and thus work out the kinks on groups of unsuspecting authors.

And to everyone who took the course, near or far, I appreciate your enthusiasm and feedback.

Finally, thanks to Shelley Bates of Moonshell Books who stepped up to copy edit this mess, even though it's not normally her jam.

AUTHOR'S NOTE

Thank you so much for reading. If you enjoyed this book, please say so in a review. I'm grateful for the time you take to do so.

I have a silly gossipy newsletter about my fiction books, called the Chirrup. I promise: no spam, no fowl. (Well, maybe a little wicker fowl and lots of giveaways and sneak peeks.) Find it and more at…

gailcarriger.com

ABOUT THE AUTHOR

Gail Carriger writes heroine's journeys that are also comedies of manners mixed with steampunk and urban fantasy (plus sexy queer romance as G L Carriger). Her books include the Parasol Protectorate, Custard Protocol, Tinkered Stars, and San Andreas Shifter series for adults, and the Finishing School series for young adults.

She is published in many languages, has over a million books in print, over a dozen *New York Times* and *USA Today* bestsellers, and starred reviews in *Publishers Weekly*, *Booklist*, *Kirkus*, and *RT Book Reviews*.

Her debut made Audible's Best list, was a Publishers Weekly Best Book, an IndieBound Notable, and a Locus Recommended Read. She has received the ALA's Alex Award, the Prix Julia Verlanger, the Elbakin Award, the Steampunk Chronicle's Reader's Choice Award, and a Starburner Award. She was once an archaeologist and is fond of shoes, cephalopods, and tea.

FICTION BY CARRIGER

AS GAIL CARRIGER

The Delightfully Deadly Stories
The Supernatural Society Stories
The Claw & Courtship Stories
The Finishing School Series
The Parasol Protectorate Series
The Custard Protocol Series

AS G. L. CARRIGER

The Tinkered Stars Series
The San Andreas Shifters Series

Made in the USA
Coppell, TX
22 August 2021

61000795R00177